Screen Printing

Screen Printing

The Beginner's Guide

Sarah Hollebone

Adam & Charles Black · London

Hollebone, Sarah
    Screen printing.
    1. Screen process printing –
      Amateurs' manuals
    I. Title
    764′.8   TT273
    ISBN 0–7136–2047–1

First published 1980
by A & C Black (Publishers) Ltd
35 Bedford Row London WC1R 4JH
© 1980 Sarah Hollebone

ISBN 0 7136 2047 1

Set, printed and bound in Great
Britain by
Fakenham Press Limited, Fakenham,
Norfolk

Contents

DEDICATION
For my family

Introduction

What is screen printing?

Screen printing is a method by which an image can be printed any number of times on paper, textiles and many other materials by squeezing ink through a stencil, which is attached to a fine mesh stretched over a rigid frame. The practical purpose of the operation is reproduction, which can amount to mass production.

Screen printing has greater versatility than many other printing methods, with applications ranging from the factory, using highly mechanised techniques, to the home and classroom where simpler hand printing methods are employed. It can, for example, be applied to articles as diverse as oil drums, tablecloths and Christmas cards. The Japanese innovators, looking forward across three centuries, might well be astonished at some of our contemporary adaptations of the medium.

This book does not attempt to cover all the possibilities, but will discuss the simpler hand printing methods, suitable for the classroom, studio or home.

What is special about the medium?

There is no such thing as a typical screen print, as the collection of plates in this book shows. Although in execution the physical precision is demanding, the variety of possibilities in style, interpretation and handling are numerous. The printer may wish to produce a formal design or be spontaneous and free, to draw intricate fine lines, create flat areas of even colour or unusual texture effects. There are suitable stencil materials that will enable him to achieve all these and many other effects. The range of inks, too, is versatile enough to enable the printer to produce anything from the powerfully brilliant and opaque to the subtle delicacy of a water colour. It is this versatility within the medium as well as its numerous uses that makes it so exciting and stimulating. For those who enjoy experimenting it is a delight, and after achieving some familiarity with the different techniques people often discover unsuspected creative resources within themselves.

What uses can screen printing be put to within the range of techniques described in this book?

The printer can produce limited editions of paper prints, which is a good way of making available original works of art at a price which is likely to be within the range of quite a large number of people. Posters are often in demand (oil based inks will stand up to exposure out of doors); Christmas cards are another obvious use and there are decorative items such as wall friezes.

Fabric can be printed for dress lengths, curtains,

bedspreads, individual decorative wall hangings, blinds, cushion covers, table mats and the ever-popular tee shirts. More unusual objects such as wooden trays, polystyrene and ceramic tiles and mirrors can also be printed. If there is a special surface that the printer wants to decorate, it is quite likely that within the extensive range available there will be a suitable ink and stencil material.

Is screen printing expensive to set up?

This can only be regarded in relative terms. The outlay is considerably less than for lithography or etching where an expensive press is required. As will be seen, a lot of the necessary equipment can be made up at home and this can mean an enormous saving. The main outlay is likely to be on inks, which should be bought in bulk wherever possible for maximum economy. All artist's equipment seems expensive today, but it is possible to use a certain amount of non-specialist improvised material in screen printing, which helps to keep costs down.

Are the techniques involved difficult to master?

It will take time to become skilful, but very little time to start enjoying yourself. Screen printing is only to be approached in the same way as one would approach the learning of any other skill or craft, by taking it slowly, step by step, starting with something not too ambitious and not expecting superb results too soon. It can be very disappointing, after the fairly laborious preparations that have to be made, when the big moment arrives and one can start the printing, only to find that time after time the beautiful image one was expecting appears marred with flaws. The important thing then, of course, is to find out what is wrong and why – and deal with the problem. A lot of time should be spent in the early stages just getting the feel of printing without minding too much what comes out. Inevitably useful discoveries are made all the time.

The key to successful printing is careful preparation at every stage from the beginning: the making of the screen, the application of the stencil, the organising of the work area, the mixing of the ink. It is a matter of being in control and never in a hurry and having the equipment in good condition.

It is not necessary to have previous training or experience in other fields of art in order to be able to learn screen printing. Some people who have, as they believe, very little creative ability but a strong desire to learn, become extremely competent and find no more difficulty than an experienced artist might, who comes to the craft for the first time.

Busy people find that screen printing, where time is concerned, can be fitted quite easily into the gaps between their other commitments. This is because it divides neatly into stages, and one learns how long each is likely to take. There always is a point – dictated by the process – when one must stop.

Many secondary schools now incorporate screen printing into their syllabus at VI Form level with considerable success. Younger children, in controlled situations, are also perfectly capable of producing satisfactory prints, and if it pleases them it should be encouraged.

One has to make up one's mind how high a standard to set for oneself, looking at prints of all kinds as much as possible in order to learn about other levels of expertise. A high quality would be required for commercial purposes, for example if one were selling a limited edition through a gallery. But the achieving of near perfection should not be considered an end in itself – it only matters if you want it. There is a happy medium where a good standard can be achieved without losing the fun and enjoyment of the whole activity.

Screen printing involves the kind of careful work that is ultimately extremely rewarding. In this book I have set up some guidelines based on systems and procedures that I know work. They may sound like rules; if so, remember that they are there to be adapted and broken as well as followed.

Part 1
Equipment and Materials

1. The screen

The screen is simply a wooden frame to which is attached a fine mesh material which is held rigid by being stretched across the frame and secured at the edges. You will print through the mesh by pulling the ink across it with a squeegee (fig. 1a and b). Screens can be bought ready for use or they can be made to order; or the bare frames can be bought for covering yourself. If you have a little carpentry experience it is not difficult to construct your own frames. As you may need several screens, the more that can be done yourself the more money you will save.

In many cases the stencil can be removed from the mesh when the print is finished (see section on the Stencil, p. 28) so a screen stretched with a good quality durable material can last for a very long time, through hundreds of prints and many cleanings.

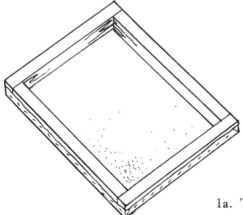

1. The frame

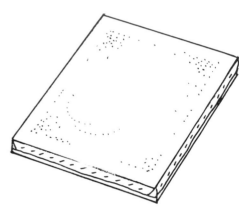

1a. The top of the screen.

1b. The bottom or underside of the screen.

When deciding upon the size of a frame, allow for a margin surrounding your picture space. This margin should be at least 10 cm (4 in.) at the top and bottom ends of the screen in order to keep the pool, or well of ink, away from the edge of the picture space and to allow for the pulling movement of the squeegee to continue freely beyond the printing area. (See pictures on p. 53 and fig. 69.) The margins at the sides of the screen can be narrower, about 5 cm (2 in.). Even if something very small such as a Christmas card is to be printed it is not advisable to use a very small screen. I would suggest 40 cm (16 in.) as the minimum length. Anything smaller restricts the freedom of movement essential to the correct handling of the squeegee, and there would be a risk of the pool of ink from the well encroaching on the picture space.

It is very important that the frame is smooth and rigid

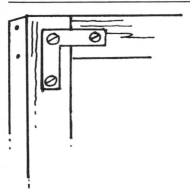

2a. A simple butt joint for making the frame.

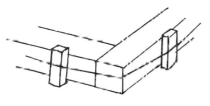

2b. String tightened with wedges holds the joints in place while the glue dries.

and lies perfectly flat. It can be constructed from any well-seasoned hardwood, the thickness of which should be chosen according to the size of the screen – the larger the screen, the sturdier the frame should be to take the strain of the tightly stretched mesh. If too light a frame is used for the size of the screen it will warp. Use the following as a guide:

For frames measuring up to 50 cm (20 in.) square use: $1\frac{1}{2} \times 1$ in. timber

For frames measuring up to 75 cm (30 in.) square use: $2 \times 1\frac{1}{2}$ in. timber

For frames measuring up to 100 cm (40 in.) square use: 2×2 in. timber

There are several ways of constructing the corner joints. Figure 2a shows the easiest. The joints are glued as shown and the frame laid down flat with a piece of strong string tied round the sides to hold the wood in position (fig. 2b). The string can be tightened by inserting wedges. Place weights on the corners and leave the glue to dry. Afterwards the pieces are nailed together with panel pins or wire nails 1 cm ($\frac{1}{8}$ in.) longer than the thickness of the wood. The joints should be reinforced on the back of the frame with metal angle brackets.

Only the more experienced carpenter should attempt the joints shown in figs. 3, 4 and 5, for which you will need a tenon saw, chisel and mitre block. All joints should be glued, as above, and when the glue is dry nail as indicated with panel pins or wire nails. No further reinforcement is needed.

3. Halving joint.

4. Open mortice and tenon joint.

5. Double open mortice and tenon joint.

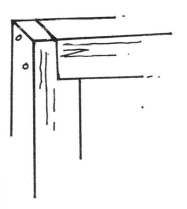

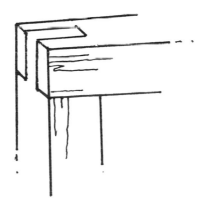

Some frames, available from specialist suppliers, can be bought in separate lengths and slotted together at the corners and then nailed and glued. The pieces are interchangeable so a variety of sizes of frame can be constructed by combining different lengths.

The completed frame should be sandpapered to a very smooth finish. The outside edge over which the mesh will be stretched must be rounded off with sandpaper to ease the stretching of the material over the edge and lessen the likelihood of tearing it.

2. The mesh

Silk is no longer exclusively used in screen printing today. It is very expensive and although it is available through some specialist suppliers, many do not stock it. Synthetic materials such as Terylene, nylon and polyester, specially manufactured for screen printing, are more commonly used and compare very well with silk for strength and durability. They come in a wide range of thicknesses. Another popular mesh material is a fine white cotton organdie – not hardwearing, but it is cheap and when waterproofed (see p. 59) is an excellent mesh for fabric printing. Another useful material, also cheaper than the specialist meshes, is polyester voile (Tergal), a curtain material. It has a relatively coarse weave, comparable to organdie, but is tougher. Both these materials are available in drapery stores.

Manufacturers of screen meshes have different ways of indicating the thickness of the material, but the supplier should be able to advise you. Sometimes the measurements are related to the silk grading system: a code number denotes the number of openings (thread count) per square inch or centimetre and one or more x's indicate the thickness of the thread. For example, 10x is a coarse weave with a fine thread and represents 43 openings (thread count of 43) per square centimetre. 10xx has the same thread count, but a slightly thicker thread. 25x is very fine and represents a thread count of 77 per square centimetre. The range, especially in the purpose-made synthetic materials, is more extensive than this, however, and it is possible to get a mesh with a thread count as high as 165 per square centimetre.

A range of 8x to 20x is usually adequate for most purposes within the scope of the hand printer. The finer the mesh, the finer your line will be. A more open mesh allows more ink through on to the printed surface. Experiment with a fine organdie or voile (these will be roughly equivalent to 8/10xx), then for a fairly fine print try a medium Terylene (or nylon) equivalent to 14x (thread count 55 per square centimetre). Having compared these you will be able to judge your further requirements.

3. Stretching the mesh

If you have a screen professionally stretched it will probably be done with a mechanical stretcher which will produce a perfectly even tension, and the mesh will be attached to the frame with a special adhesive suitable only for use with the mechanical stretching equipment. If possible, have a look at a ready made screen before making your own by hand. This will give you an idea of the degree and evenness of tension to aim for, but it is unlikely that you will achieve the standard of a mechanically stretched screen. This is not going to matter within the range of application described in this book but in the case of an exceptionally large screen (over 100 cm (40 in.) in length) it would be advisable to get it professionally stretched.

When stretching by hand the best way to secure the material is with staples. If two people work together, one holding the material in place while the other staples, the process will be easier and the result better. There are several methods, and after experimenting you will adopt the one you prefer.

Always cut along the straight in the direction of the weave of the fabric making it 5 cm (2 in.) larger all round than the size of the frame. If silk or nylon is used, damp it first.

Method 1. Stand the frame on end and fold the material over the rounded off edge, turned under as for a hem to

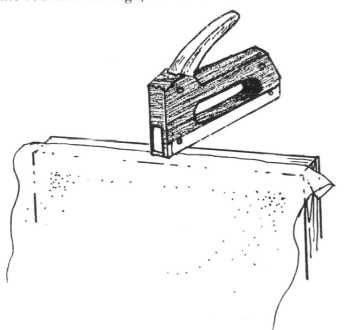

6. With the frame on end, fold the turned-under material over the edge and staple, using a staple gun.

13

Part of the way through stretching the mesh over the screen, a tension should be clearly visible going through the middle in both directions. (See dotted lines in figs. below.)

avoid fraying (fig. 6). Place two or three staples in the centre, then stretching the material hard across the frame, place three more staples in the centre of the opposite side (fig. 7). Pulling against one staple only might tear the material. Secure the material in the same way to the centres of the remaining two opposite sides. You now have a tension going across the screen through the middle in both directions

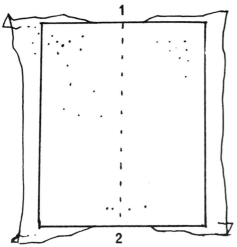

7. Staple again in the centre of the opposite side.

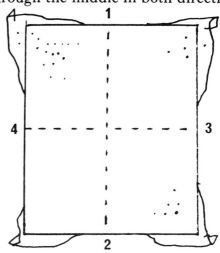

8. Staple again in the centres of the two remaining sides.

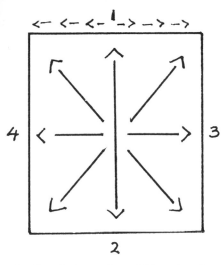

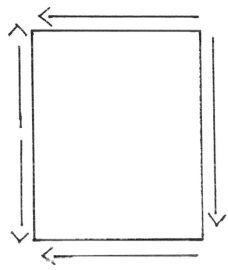

9. Staple from the middle of each side towards the corners.

10. Alternatively, staple the whole of one side first, then staple the adjacent sides in turn.

4. Hinges and baseboard

(fig. 8). Proceed along from the middle of each side towards the corners, pulling the material firmly between the opposite sides as you go (fig. 9). The staples should now be about 1 cm ($\frac{1}{2}$ in.) apart. Pull hard towards the corners to eliminate any softness or ripple and secure with several staples. Tap the mesh. It should be quite resonant and drumlike. Tidy up the edges if necessary with more staples.

Method 2. Staple the whole of one side first, starting at one end, then staple the adjacent sides, starting from the first finished side (fig. 10). The fourth side is secured from the centre outwards, so that any ripple can be worked towards the corners.

Method 3. Staple on to the underside of the frame using either stapling sequence described above. This is easier if you are stretching on your own, because the frame need not be held upright. It is obviously useful if you are short of material.

Whichever method you use, make sure that the staples are firmly embedded. Hammer them if necessary. If the screen is not stretched taut enough, undo one side and restretch. When the gumstrip is applied (p. 43, sealing the screen) the tautness will increase as the wet gumstrip dries and shrinks. However, this is no remedy for a really slack screen. The stretching process is laborious, but it is worth taking trouble over and it is encouraging to remember that the screen could last for years.

For making paper prints the screen should be attached with hinges to a baseboard that can be the same size or slightly larger than the frame. The board should be smooth and flat. $\frac{3}{4}$ in. blockboard or a fine $\frac{3}{4}$ in. chipboard are ideal. The printing paper will be laid on this board, its exact position being registered (p. 48, registration of paper prints) so that each piece of paper can be put down in precisely the same place. It is very useful to have a supporting leg attached, fairly loosely with a screw to one side of the frame, so that it will swing down and hold the screen in a raised position (not more than 30 degrees or the ink might spill out) while the paper is being removed and replaced (figs. 11 and 12).

The screen should be attached to the board with

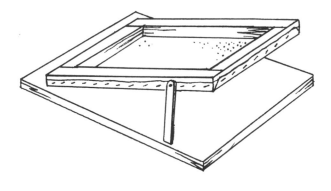

11. A supporting 'leg' will hold the screen up while the paper is being removed and replaced.

12. The screen should be attached to the baseboard by a pair of sturdy hinges.

13. Lift-off butt hinge.

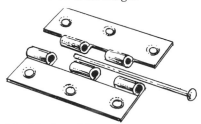

14. Pin butt hinge.

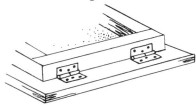

15. Hinges fixed to the top of the baseboard.

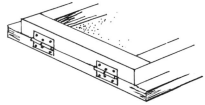

16. Hinges fixed to the back edge of the baseboard.

partable hinges, which make it very easy to detach the screen from the baseboard. Select a fairly heavy pair of good quality. One type is the lift off butt hinge (fig. 13). Make sure that the prongs do not slip out of the sockets too easily or your screen may shift and cause a misplacement of the printed image. It is important to check the hinges frequently during printing to make sure this does not happen. Another type is the pin butt hinge. This is more likely to stay in position than the lift off kind as the hinge cannot shift unless the pin is removed (fig. 14). Hinges can be fixed to the top of the board or to the back edge (figs. 15 and 16).

To fix, undo the hinges and screw two corresponding parts to the baseboard, positioned so that they will be a short distance in from the corners of the frame. See figs. 15 and 16. Slot in the second two halves and mark the positions of the screw holes against the edges of the frame. Detach and fix to frame. Rejoin the hinge parts. It is now possible to raise and lower the screen within an angle of 90 degrees. If a different screen is to be used for each colour, several sets of hinges identical with the first will be necessary, so that the appropriate parts can be fixed to each screen and their positions accurately related to those on the baseboard. Thus the screens can be easily interchanged.

For a paper print, to ensure that the printed image is crisp, the screen should not be in permanent contact with the printing paper during the printing process. The mesh should be allowed to spring away from the paper after the squeegee has crossed at any given point. Stick some pieces of card under the four corners of the underside of the screen to raise it about $\frac{1}{2}$ cm ($\frac{1}{4}$ in.). The slacker the screen, the greater the distance will have to be. This space allowance is called the 'snap-off'. The card should be fixed before the hinges are attached to the screen (fig. 17a and b).

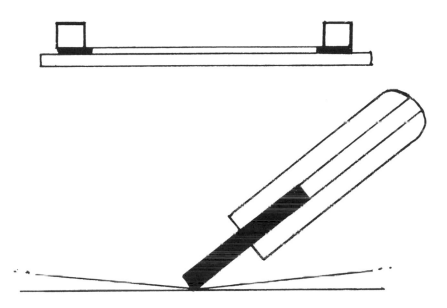

17a and b. 'Snap-off' allows the mesh to spring away from the paper when the squeegee has crossed it.

Alternatively, the screen can be joined to the baseboard by means of a hinge bar the same depth as the frame. This bar is attached to the board using coach bolts, wing nuts and washers and is adjustable vertically, thus allowing for a much easier adjustment for 'snap-off'. Another piece of the same card used under the frame can be wedged beneath the hinge bar (fig. 17c).

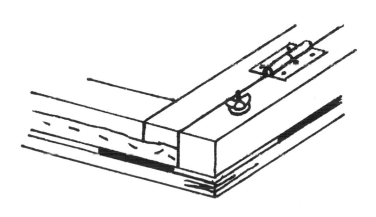

17c. The screen attached to an adjustable hinge bar.

There are inks available for a multitude of specialised purposes, and you should consult the manufacturers' catalogues.

1. Oil based inks for printing on paper and card

The most widely used are densely pigmented inks with a matt or satin finish. They are opaque straight from the tin but can be mixed with an extender base (sometimes called a 'reducer') which makes them transparent. Ink always needs thinning down with turpentine or white spirit to achieve the correct consistency for printing (p. 52, printing). Colours can of course be mixed together but not if they are the products of different manufacturers – they may vary slightly in consistency and composition. There is no reason, however, why they should not be *over*printed once they are *completely* dry.

Other finishes obtainable are high-gloss and fluorescent. There is also a range of inks known as trichromatic, consisting of the three spectrum primary colours (cyan, magenta and yellow) accompanied by black and a special extender base. These are completely transparent and produce very beautiful translucent effects. The colours are much stronger than those formed by the mixture of the regular ink with extender. (See plate 14b in the colour section.)

Metallic finishes can be obtained in powder form and mixed with a special binding medium.

Any of these inks can be used in conjunction with each other by overprinting, achieving some fascinating effects. They are all soluble with turpentine or white spirit which is generally used for cleaning as well as thinning. On occasions a stronger cleaner is needed, especially if ink has begun to dry in the screen. These can be obtained from hardware stores, and all manufacturers of screen inks have their own recommended solvents. Special screen sprays are available which effectively declog the screen. This is very useful if any drying out occurs during printing (p. 56, faults 2). It may occasionally be necessary, in excessively hot, dry conditions, to add a retarder to the ink to slow down the drying process. Conversely, to speed up drying, an accelerator can be added. In either case, any leftover ink with which they have been mixed is not worth keeping for future use.

It is usually more economical to buy large size tins of ink. Ink will keep a long while as long as the lids are sealed down really tightly after use. If the lid has become misshapen and lets in air, wrap a piece of tin foil over the opening and press the lid firmly down, or pour a little white spirit into the top of the tin.

Inks that have been mixed can be stored in screw top jars or old tins for future use. Yogurt or cream cartons are only suitable for very short term use as containers – the ink will dissolve the container in a matter of hours.

Stencils used must be resistant to these inks and solvents (see p. 29, the stencil). Suitable stencil materials are paper, profilm, greenfilm and other water soluble film, glue and photographic stencils.

2. Water soluble inks for printing on paper or card

You can make yourself an ink out of a mixture of powder paint and wallpaper paste: dissolve the paste powder according to instructions as for normal weight wallpaper, and add the powder colour. It will dissolve in the paste as you stir.

Instead of powder paint, cold water dye can be added to the paste. Powder dye should first be dissolved in a little hot water.

Gum arabic can be used as a binder as an alternative to wallpaper paste. This can be obtained in crystal or powder form. The proportions are one pound of gum to two pints of water. Crystals should be soaked overnight in the cold water, then slowly brought to the boil with constant stirring. Cool and strain before use to remove any impurities. The powder is added to the cold water, then slowly brought to the boil. It should be left for several hours before use.

These inks have a very different appearance from the oil based ones, having a special quality of their own. Unlike oil based inks, which form a film on the surface of the paper, these sink in. They are transparent, unless an opaque white is added, giving scope for overprinted effects.

The gum arabic mixture will keep in a jar with a tight fitting lid, but wallpaper paste will start to decompose after a few days.

There are inks specially produced for printing on paper, emulsion based and ready for use. Water soluble block-printing emulsion with a little water added is also recommended.

None of the inks mentioned above should be used for printing on fabric, but all screen printing fabric inks (see below) are suitable and very effective for printing on paper. Fixing additives are not necessary. Cold water is used for washing screens and tools immediately after use.

The stencils used with these inks must be water resistant. Suitable stencil materials are waxed paper, waterproofed or water resistant film, wax, shellac, and photographic stencils. Ordinary paper stencils can be used for 'one-off' prints.

3. Inks for printing on fabric

These consist of pigment, bound in a water soluble emulsion, plus a substance that enables the colour to be fixed permanently into the fabric after curing.

Some ranges of ink come ready mixed. Some come ready mixed apart from the catalyst (fixing substance) which is added before use. Some come with separate binder, already containing catalyst, and special liquid tinters. Some come with binder, tinters and catalyst separately. Curing methods vary (see p. 72, curing) with the different products.

The storage potential of the inks is limited once the catalyst is added; recommended storage life ranges from days to months according to the product.

The binder is white, though not opaque, so the colours are transparent unless mixed with opaque white. The consistency is like thick cream, right for printing as it comes and no water should be added.

The tinters are very powerful and are added to the binder in small drops. The consistency of the binder is only minutely affected by the addition of tinters and catalyst. Gold and silver powder can be mixed with a special binder. (See the table mats in plate 13 in the colour section.) The powder must first be dissolved and mixed into a paste. Fluorescent colours are also obtainable.

There are some multi-purpose inks recommended for a variety of techniques such as block-printing, batik, or direct painting onto fabric. They will generally have to be adapted for screen printing by being added to a thickener or to an extender, according to the manufacturer's instructions.

Screens and tools are washed with cold water immediately after use. There are also special solvents which may be necessary if the ink has hardened in the screen mesh.

Mixed inks should be stored in jars (not tins) or in plastic containers with tight fitting lids.

Suitable stencil materials are waterproofed or water resistant film, wax, shellac and photographic stencils. Paper can be used for 'one-off' prints, waxed paper for longer runs.

4. Inks for other special purposes

Wood and hardboard. Plastic or cellulose gloss screen inks are recommended, but study manufacturers' leaflets before making your choice. These inks give off a powerful smell and can cause harmful irritation. It is essential to use them in a very well-ventilated area. They have their own special solvents.

Suitable stencil material: paper, water soluble film, liquid glue and photographic stencils.

Oil based inks can also be used and can be varnished over afterwards. (See p. 19 for stencil material, and p. 18 for information on oil based inks.)

Wood should be treated with a sealer before printing.

Glass, metal and glazed ceramic tiles. A hard gloss screen ink is recommended. There are several types including a two-pack system where a catalyst is added to the coloured base before use. Some are soluble with white spirit, others have special solvents. As with those mentioned above it would be advisable to consult manufacturers' leaflets.

Experience shows that when some printed objects are exposed to a lot of steam and frequent washing, for instance glazed ceramic tiles used in a bathroom or shower or round a kitchen sink, the ink tends eventually to flake. They should therefore be used for decorative purposes in a more protected position and not washed too often.

Suitable stencil material: paper, water soluble film, glue and photographic stencils.

PVC (rigid or flexible). Use plastic based gloss inks. See above.

Polystyrene. Use oil based inks. A special thinner may be recommended to achieve really good adhesion.

5. Storage and care of inks

All screen inks should be stored in a cool place protected from frost and direct sunlight. Many are inflammable and some are toxic and cause irritation to skin, eyes and respiratory system. Some give off unpleasant smells – screen printing should always be carried out in a well ventilated area. Detailed information can be obtained from manufacturers' leaflets which should be studied carefully. Great care must be taken in selecting inks for children to use.

3. The Squeegee

The squeegee is the tool which is used to draw the ink across the screen, squeezing it through the mesh (see figs. 18, 19 and 20, and the pictures on p. 53).

The blade of the squeegee is either rubber or plastic and can vary in sharpness and flexibility. The choice of blade is very largely a matter of personal preference. A hard, sharp blade is best suited to fine work and a thin deposit of paint. A fairly flexible sharp blade will serve all but the most extreme requirements. There is not much to choose between a polyurethane blade and a good quality rubber one. The former is more expensive but more durable and less likely to be eroded by some of the chemicals contained in the inks and solvents. A good quality rubber blade, if carefully cleaned straight after use, will prove to be very good value. Beware of poor quality rubber, which will crack and crumble at the blade edge. It is not easy to tell the quality – make careful enquiries before you buy.

The blade is fixed into a handle, usually wooden, and can be removed and replaced. Squeegees can be bought from suppliers of screen printing materials who also supply handles and lengths of rubber or plastic blade in several standard sizes for assembling yourself. You are likely to need several squeegees because the sizes of your prints and screens will vary. There should be at least half an inch to spare between the ends of the squeegee and the edge of the frame and the squeegee should be at least an inch wider than the printing space (fig. 21).

If the blade becomes blunted after much use, or the edge deteriorates in any way, it can be sharpened by rubbing along a strip of sandpaper which is attached to a piece of wood. This device ensures that the blade will be sharpened evenly (fig. 22). If a very tiny area (not more than $5\frac{1}{2}$ cm or 2 in. square) has to be printed, a small piece of blade held in the hand will be quite adequate.

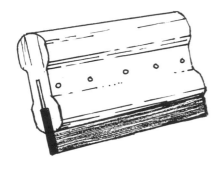

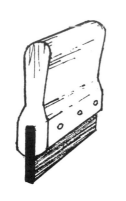

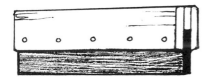

18, 19 and 20. Various types of squeegee, the tool used to draw the ink across the mesh.

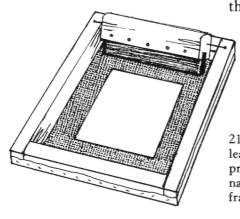

21. The squeegee should be at least an inch wider than the printing space, and an inch narrower than the width of the frame.

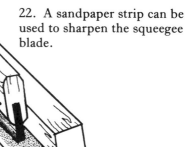

22. A sandpaper strip can be used to sharpen the squeegee blade.

Constructing your own squeegee

23. Screws used in constructing a squeegee.

To make a squeegee using a blade 37 cm (15 in.) × 5 cm (2 in.) × 9 mm ($\frac{3}{8}$ in.) you will need one piece of wood (preferably hardwood) 37 cm (15 in.) × 5 cm (2 in.) × 9 mm ($\frac{3}{8}$ in.), and two pieces of wood 37 cm (15 in.) × 7.5 cm (3 in.) × 9 mm ($\frac{3}{8}$ in.). Round headed screws with washers and nuts *or* saw screws are also needed (fig. 23). Get brass screws if possible to avoid rusting.

Construct the wooden handle first, aligning the three lengths along one edge and sandwiching the smaller between the larger two (figs. 24, 25 and 26). Glue the pieces together and clamp in position until dry. Plane or sandpaper the grip area to a comfortable rounded shape. The squeegee is likely to be washed frequently, so protect the wood by sealing it with at least two coats of polyurethane varnish before inserting the blade.

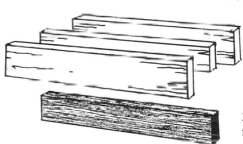
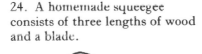

24. A homemade squeegee consists of three lengths of wood and a blade.

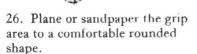

25. Construct the wooden handle first.

26. Plane or sandpaper the grip area to a comfortable rounded shape.

When the varnish is dry, insert the blade and drill holes to fit the screws through the wood and the blade. Holes should be not more than 12.5 cm (5 in.) apart (fig. 27). A long nail or screw at each end of the handle will allow the squeegee to rest against the edge of the frame without falling into the ink well (fig. 28).

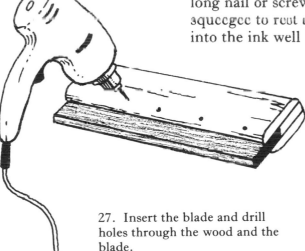

27. Insert the blade and drill holes through the wood and the blade.

28. A long screw at each end of the handle will allow the squeegee to rest against the edge of the frame.

4. The printer's table and work area

One of the most important requirements for efficient screen printing is space, not such an easy commodity to come by. The ideal would be a room given over to the purpose, but you could manage in the average kitchen. Take a lot of trouble organising your space and equipment.

For paper printing you need a table with enough space for your baseboard and screen in the centre, room on one side for your jars of ink, thinning and cleaning equipment, palette, etc. and room on the other side for the pile of printing paper so that each new piece is instantly to hand to be placed under the screen as soon as the last one is removed (fig. 29).

There should be space nearby to lay out or hang wet prints.

29. The work area should be well organised, with all equipment conveniently to hand.

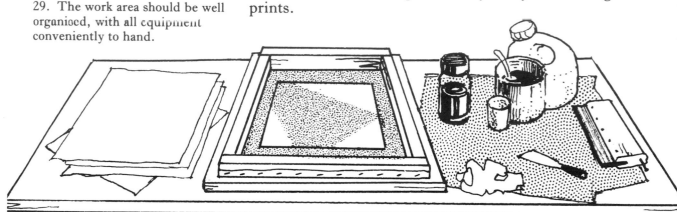

1. The work surface for paper printing

If you have a small but sturdy table and wish to enlarge it, this can easily be done by laying a suitably large piece of blockboard onto the original top and screwing it down. If you are using a kitchen table to work on, or indeed any table not given over exclusively to your print-making, cover the top with a strong PVC or rubber cloth. Printing inks and their solvents and cleaners will stain and discolour and remove polish.

2. The work surface for fabric printing

The surface must be smooth and firm and slightly flexible. For a permanent printing area the table should be covered with a thick blanket or carpet felt, stretched out tightly so that there are no creases, and tacked to the edge of the table. Over this should be laid a washable sheet of PVC or vinyl which again must be smoothed and tacked down over the table edges. A vinyl covering as used in upholstery, with a soft backing, is very suitable (fig. 30). A single board –

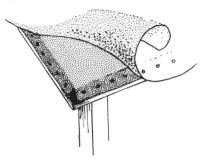

30. The work surface for fabric printing, covered with soft-backed upholstery vinyl.

blockboard, chipboard or ply – could be covered in the same way and used as a removable fabric printing surface.

You can use your permanent fabric printing work top when you are printing on paper because you will be using a baseboard. (Never carry out a paper print on a soft surface; conversely, never print fabric over a hard surface.) Use a tray or board to stand the jars of paint, etc. on.

3. Drying equipment

Paper prints where oil based inks have been used will be touch-dry within an hour, but should not be stacked up for several hours. The time taken to dry completely depends on the atmosphere, the ink, and the number of layers of colour that have been printed. Water soluble inks dry much faster.

The simplest drying device is a line of strong string to which the prints can be pegged like washing. They can be hung in pairs, back to back (fig. 31), or, to make better use of the line space, the string can be threaded through holes bored in the tops of the pegs, so that the prints can hang across the line (fig. 32). Hang them singly, all facing in the same direction in case draughts blow them together (fig. 33).

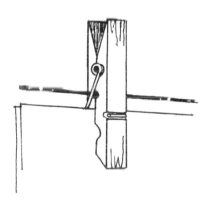

31. Prints can be pegged up in pairs, back to back.

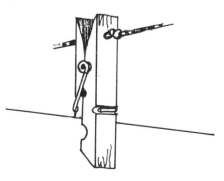

32. Alternatively, thread the line through holes bored in the top of the pegs to save space.

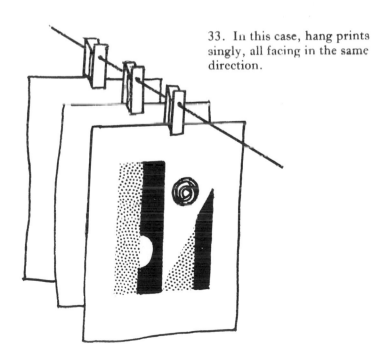

33. In this case, hang prints singly, all facing in the same direction.

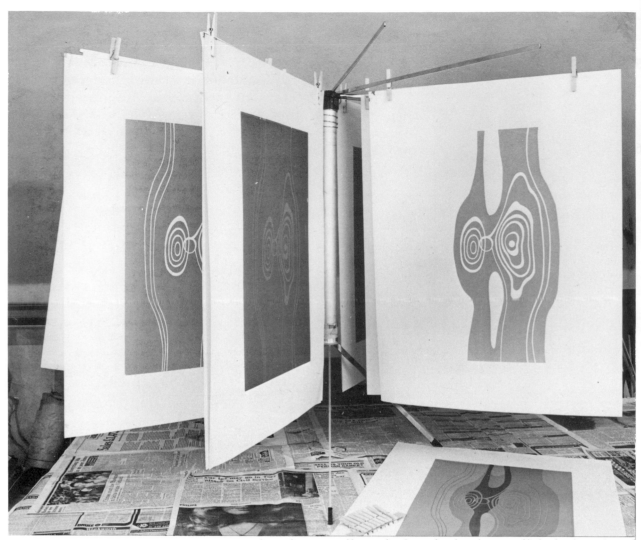

A radial clothes dryer is ideal for drying prints.

Another excellent drying device is a radial clothes dryer. This stands on the floor and the prints are clipped on with clothes pegs. When not in use the rack can be folded and stacked away.

For the classroom or large studio, there are purpose-made racks for drying large numbers of prints. When dry, the prints, unless mounted, should be kept flat. It is possible to buy very large polythene envelopes which will hold up to 40 sheets of medium weight cartridge paper stacked up.

For fabric prints the clothes line is the obvious place for drying most articles. Very large pieces are best left on the printing table until dry.

4. Washing equipment

A large sink or bath is best when washing out a screen. If there is no hand spray, attach a piece of garden hosepipe to the cold tap.

5. Storage space It is important to have a fairly cool, well protected place, *not* the larder, with shelves if possible to store the tins and jars of ink and the solvents and cleaners. (See p. 21, storage and care of inks.)

6. Miscellaneous articles Screw top jars and tins with lids for storing ink.
Palette knives (kitchen type) for mixing colours.
Cheap metal spoons.
Palette (plate or tin lid).
Absorbent rag and kitchen paper.
Old newspaper.
Coating trough for scraping liquid stencil over the screen (see page 35).
Fan heater or blow dryer for drying stencils and screens.

5. Printing paper

There is an enormous range of paper, varying in colour, texture, finish and price, that is suitable for screen printing. It is a matter of personal choice.

Experimenting with different papers is very enjoyable. Look at all the papers available in art material shops and stationers. Try out prints on blotting paper, newspaper, textured and patterned paper. (See plates 15 and 19, no. 3.) Cellophane and paper with metallic finishes can be printed on. For the purest colour production, absolutely white paper is best.

Just about any paper can be printed on with oil based ink, but extremely smooth non-porous surfaces (papers with metallic finishes, cellophane, etc.) are not suitable for water soluble inks. Very lightweight papers should also be avoided when using water soluble inks, as they may buckle and shrink.

For stencil paper see p. 29, paper stencils.

Part 2
The Stencil

34. The stencil.

35. The image produced by working colour through the open parts of the stencil.

1. Paper stencils

The stencil is the means by which your design is translated into a print. Making it is certainly one of the most creative and fascinating aspects of the whole process.

Basically, stencilling is a method of reproducing an image by the use of a cut-out shape in a thin, flat material. Most of us are familiar with the use of simple stencils from childhood. This cut-out, or stencil, is laid on to the surface on which the design is to be imprinted and colour is worked through the open parts; the material surrounding the open spaces forms a barrier, or resist, which prevents the colour from being imprinted on the areas where it is not wanted (figs. 34 and 35). This process can be repeated to reproduce the image many more times. In screen printing the stencil is held in position by being attached to the mesh of the screen. There are many kinds of stencil that can be used, each having its own character suitable to different types of design. As you become more experienced you will be able to build up a print using a combination of two or more kinds of stencil. (See plates 1, 12 and 13, no. 2 in colour section.) It is essential that the stencil material selected is not adversely affected by the inks and solvents being used.

The paper stencil is the easiest to make and is a good one to start practising with. Use it when a simple design is planned. An intricate design in paper is difficult to handle and may tear before it is finally attached to the screen. Suitable papers are tracing paper, greaseproof paper, layout paper, thin cartridge paper, newspaper. The obvious advantage of transparent paper is that you can lay it over your master design and trace straight on to the stencil.

If the paper stencil is to be used with water soluble inks, duplicates will have to be made and a new one applied for each printing, because the ink will soak into the paper and cause it to crinkle and become saturated so that it is no longer effective as a resist (see p. 59, printing on fabric). It is useful for 'one-off' prints.

There is a specially prepared stencil paper, suitable for use with water soluble inks. This is coated on one side with wax and lasts considerably longer than ordinary paper. It can also be peeled off the stencil and wiped clean with a damp cloth, and used again for a change of colour. The waxed side is placed against the screen mesh.

Oil based inks will not penetrate the paper so the same stencil can be used a number of times. How long the paper will last before beginning to disintegrate depends on various factors, such as the strength of the paper and how much ink is coming through the mesh.

It must be remembered when using oil based inks that the stencil will be destroyed when the screen is cleaned after printing each different colour, so if you wish to print some copies using a different colour scheme you will have to have duplicates of the stencil.

The paper can be cut with scissors or a blade (a stencil knife) giving a hard, sharp edge, or torn if an irregular soft edge is required. It can also be treated to give a texture (see page 76, textures). Several layers can be cut at the same time when making duplicates.

Stencils are always attached to the *underside* of the screen so that they are not harmed by the action of the squeegee pulling the ink across the mesh. A small paper stencil will attach itself to the screen when the first ink is drawn across and should remain firmly stuck by the ink. It can be pulled off without any difficulty. A larger piece of stencil paper – particularly if it is of the heavier type – needs to be attached to the screen first, either with a few dabs of glue or small pieces of sticky tape (figs. 36, 37 and 38). To remove a paper stencil, simply peel off.

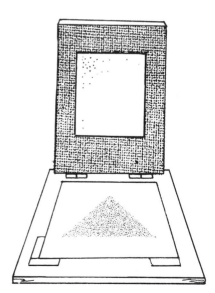

36. The stencil should be attached to the underside of the screen.

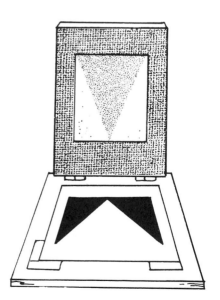

37. A small paper stencil will attach itself to the screen when the first ink is drawn across.

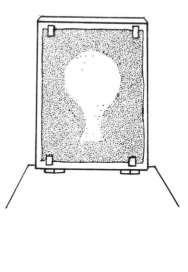

38. A larger stencil should be attached to the screen first, with glue or sticky tape.

Placing a small paper stencil on the
sheet of printing paper.

When the ink has been drawn
across, this paper stencil will stick
firmly to the screen ready for the
next print.

2. Film stencils

These are more reliable than paper stencils because they are
stronger and last longer, and they are suitable for more
elaborate designs. They are stuck down on to the mesh and
can only be removed with appropriate solvents. Used
correctly, with inks compatible with the stencil material,
they will not be affected by the ink solvents and cleaners,
and can therefore be used with any number of colour
changes. When you buy the film it is attached to a backing
material which is peeled off after the stencil has been stuck to
the mesh. There are quite a lot of different types of film
stencil on the market for use with different types of ink, and
some of the more popular ones are described below.

Profilm (Stenplex Amber). This is suitable for use with oil
based inks, and it can also be used with water soluble inks
for short runs. Used with water soluble inks it will last better
if waterproofed (see p. 59, preparing the screen for fabric
printing). It will adhere very well to natural fibre meshes,
less well to synthetics. I have however used it quite
successfully with Terylene and polyester.

Lay the sheet of profilm over your master design, film
(shiny) side up. Work on a firm surface and secure the

39. Stencil cutting blades.

profilm with sticky tape or drawing pins so that it does not slip. Stencil cutters are generally used to cut the design out of the film. These consist of a holder into which a variety of shapes of blade can be inserted (fig. 39). There are also pairs of compasses which have a blade point, which are very useful for geometric patterns. Straight lines should be cut against a metal ruler. Cut carefully round the outline of the shapes that are to be printed, cutting through the film only and *not* the paper backing (fig. 40). Remove the cut out pieces of film leaving the sheet backing intact. The blade must be very

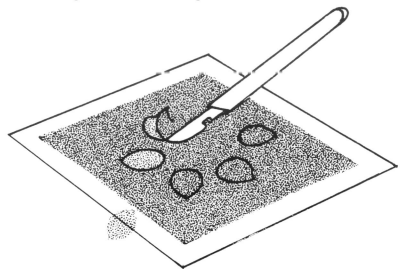

40. Cut through the film only, not the paper backing.

sharp – if it is blunt you will get messy edges. You should make the most of the clean, sharp lines so characteristic of this type of stencil (see plate 20, no. 4).

Having cut the design the next step is to attach the film to the underside of the screen by pressing it with a hot iron. The heat will melt the shiny film, which is basically a layer of shellac, and so transfer it to the mesh.

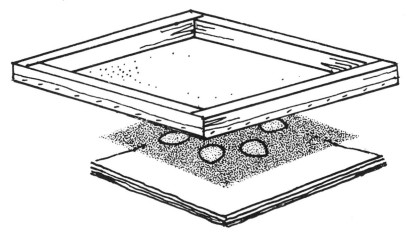

41. Lay the film right side up on a pad of newspapers, and put the screen on top.

Plate 1, right. 'Woodgrain.' This design was developed from a wood rubbing, and was printed using a combination of liquid and paper stencil. Liquid glue was used to form lines, and paper stencil for the flat areas of colour. See plate 22 for the first stage of this print.

Plate 2, below. 'Girls Shelling Peas.' An original photograph was used to make three tone separations and three separate photographic stencils. The three layers were printed over a coloured background.

Plate 3, top left. 'White Cliff.' This shows the use of cut and torn paper stencils.

Plates 4 and 5, far left and left. 'Cockerels.' Freely adapted from a 7th-century Sassanian woven silk design. The final layer was overprinted with a pattern of clear polyurethane varnish, the rest of the print having a matt finish. Gold ink was used in the design for extra richness.

Plate 6, above. 'Red Planet.' Incompatible substances, water soluble glue (Autotype Blue screen filler) and white spirit, were pressed between two pieces of heavy duty plastic sheeting. The resultant mottled foundation of glue was transferred to the screen by pressing one of the plastic sheets on to it. The print was built up in layers, using the same screen.

Plate 7, above. 'Ponte Vecchio, Florence.' This print was built up using liquid stencil (Autotype Blue screen filler) and overprinted in many layers using the same screen.

Plate 8, right. 'Apples.' Ink has been mixed with extender to create transparent colours which have been very effectively overprinted.

Plate 9, left. 'Sunburst.'
Here is an interesting play
between different shades of
the same colour, and
transparent and opaque
inks. Note the frame, where
opaque is blended into
transparent colour.

Plate 10, below. 'Moving
Figure.' A photographic
stencil made from an
original line drawing.
Several overprintings were
made using the same
stencil, offset to create a
feeling of movement.

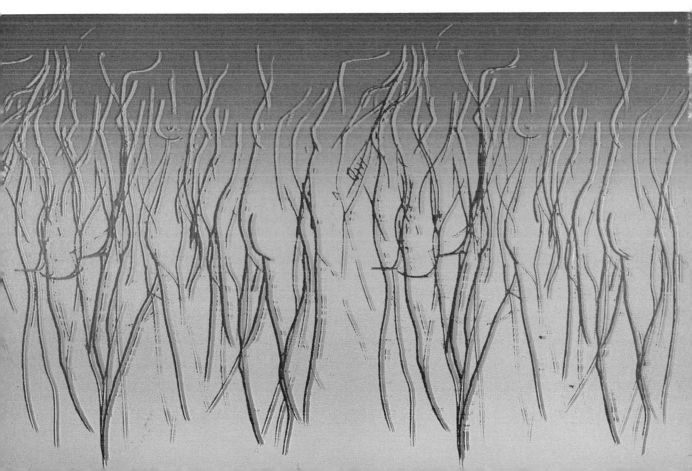

Plate 11, left. 'Balloon.' The roundness of the balloon was achieved with a blend of transparent and opaque inks overprinted with pulls going across in several directions. The background contains some subtle blends.

Plate 12, below. 'Geraniums.' A combination of photographic stencil – for the shadow and positive leaf shapes – and cut paper stencils has been used to create this lively print.

Plate 13, opposite.

1. 'Market Place'. Carefully pre-planned overprinting of colours in different sequences gives a rich range of shades from relatively few basic colours.

2. 'Zebras' is a one-off wall hanging printed on calico, using a combination of cut film and paper stencils.

3. 'Butterflies.' A deliberately unmixed blend of inks on the butterflies' wings gives a streaky, tortoiseshell effect.

4 and 5. Plain coloured silk squares, printed with four repeats all fitted together on the same screen. Both squares use the same stencil, the blue version being overprinted so that the pattern is offset.

6. Tablemats printed on coloured hessian using gold ink. The designs are adapted from a Columbian gold motif.

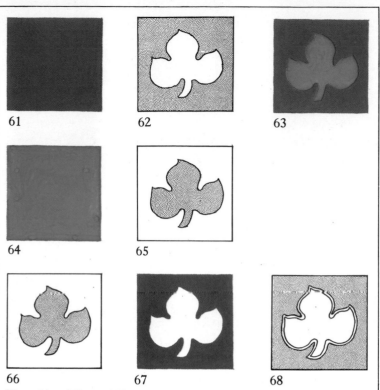

61. Background colour is printed first through the open rectangle.

62. The stencil, with open central area.

63. The second colour, in this case green, is printed through the stencil.

64. This time the green is printed through the open rectangle.

65. In this case the positive leaf shape is used as the resist, and the orange is overprinted, but the result is the same as fig 63.

66. In the third method the positive leaf shape is used again as the resist.

67. The first printing is done over the positive stencil, resulting in an orange rectangle with white central figure.

68. The second stencil is used with the figure slightly larger than the designed size, to give an overlap.

Plate 14a. Three different ways in which to achieve a green leaf shape printed on an orange background.

Plate 14b, above. Different effects that can be achieved by overprinting with transparent cyan, magenta and yellow inks. The shades vary subtly according to the order in which they are printed.

Plate 14c, left. Blue glue stencil being built up stage by stage on the same screen, and the resultant prints. On the left are the three stages in building up the stencil, on the right the way the print develops with application of three colours.

The screen must be thoroughly clean – any residual oiliness from previous use may prevent the film from sticking properly. (See page 58, cleaning up.) Lay the film right side up on a firm surface on top of a pad of newspapers evenly laid for consistent contact – this is to push the stencil tightly against the mesh and give a nice padded base for ironing over (figs. 41 and 42). Lay the screen down on top of your

42. This pushes the stencil against the mesh and provides a firm base for ironing over.

43. When the film is securely stuck, peel off the backing paper.

stencil, then place a piece of thin paper over the mesh. Heat the iron to silk pressing temperature and keep it moving constantly over the stencil area. Quite quickly the film will start to melt and stick, indicated by a slight darkening and glistening (just visible through the mesh), and the backing paper becomes mottled as it separates from the film. Gently pull a corner of the backing paper. If it comes away easily, leaving the film behind firmly attached to the mesh, you have ironed enough. If the backing paper pulls the film away, continue to iron. Be very cautious – over-heating may result in the film melting into the backing paper, or becoming so firmly embedded into the mesh that it becomes almost impossible to remove. When you are satisfied that the film is stuck all over, peel off all the backing paper (fig 43).

To remove a profilm stencil, first remove ink with appropriate cleaners, then lay the screen down on a sheet of polythene and flood with methylated spirits. After a few minutes the film will peel off quite easily. Stubborn particles can be scratched off.

Greenfilm (Stenplex Green). This is similar to profilm, but it adheres very well to all synthetic meshes. It is water soluble, so cannot be used with water soluble inks at all unless waterproofed (see p. 59, preparing the screen for fabric printing). It is cut in exactly the same way as profilm.

To attach it to the mesh, lay the cut film on a pad of paper with the screen on top. Take a piece of cotton wool saturated with three parts methylated spirits to one part water, and squeeze out thoroughly. The addition of the meths to the water reduces through evaporation the amount of moisture reaching the film and ensures that it will not be

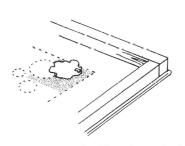

44. Dampen the film through the mesh with a piece of cotton wool soaked in meths and water.

over-wetted. Dampen the film through the mesh by pressing hard with the moist cotton wool, taking an area of about 30 cm × 30 cm (12 in. × 12 in.) at a time (fig. 44). Immediately place a piece of brown paper, shiny side down, on to the treated area and iron with the setting at silk pressing temperature. As with profilm, the change in appearance as the film adheres will be visible through the mesh. Continue to treat the screen section by section until the whole stencil has been transferred, then peel off the backing paper.

To remove a greenfilm stencil, first remove ink with appropriate cleaners, then soak in hot water.

Autocut. This is a water soluble stencil not suitable for use with water soluble inks. It is cut in the same way as the other film stencils described above. To attach it to the mesh, place the stencil on a pad of paper, put the screen on top of it and wipe over quickly and evenly with a sponge soaked in water. Blot away the excess water. The screen should now be dried in a warm place – or better, use a fan heater or blow dryer. Remove the backing film when completely dry. No ironing is necessary. The stencil is removed by spraying hard with cold water.

Red Mask. This is a red film backed with a transparent plastic sheet. It is impervious to both water and white spirit, and can therefore be used with oil or water based inks. It is soluble with acetone. It can also be used for making hand-cut photo positives (see page 38, photographic stencils). It is cut in the same way as the other film stencils.

Lay the cut stencil on a firm pad of paper under the screen, and with a wad of cotton wool soaked in acetone and squeezed out, rub through the mesh onto the film, taking in a very small area at a time (about 15 cm × 15 cm, 6 in. × 6 in.). The film dissolves very quickly. Have some blotting paper ready and soak up the excess moisture before any dissolved film runs into the open mesh. Continue to treat the stencil in this way, section by section, then peel off the backing paper.

To remove the stencil, soak in acetone.

3. Directly applied stencils

These are painted or drawn straight on to the mesh, the area covered forming the resist. A very exciting range of effects can be created (see p. 76, textures).

Glue. One of the most versatile and pleasant substances to use is a water soluble glue suitable for use with oil based inks. This has colour added so that it can be seen clearly when being applied to the screen. There are glues specially prepared for the purpose, obtainable from suppliers of screen printing materials. They are sometimes referred to as 'fillers', and must not be confused with another type of filler which is not suitable for stencils because it is difficult to manipulate and impossible to remove when dry. Check with the supplier that you are buying the right product. Ordinary water soluble gum can also be used (e.g. Gloy gum and gum arabic).

Use a mesh in the fine to medium range – a coarse mesh will not fill so efficiently and you may get a saw-tooth edge.

If you apply the glue with a brush, you will be able to get a far more flexible line than with paper or film stencils. You can work spontaneously or to a pre-planned design. If you are working to a design, make a drawing of it the size you want it to be, place your screen on top of it and trace the design onto the mesh with a soft pencil, then fill in with glue. Cover the pencil line so that traces of lead do not get into the ink and make dirty streaks on the print. Raise the screen slightly so that the mesh is not touching the table surface while glue is being applied.

45a. The coating trough.

45b. Applying glue using the coating trough.

You are in fact painting a *negative*, blocking out the areas you wish to remain unprinted. You can use the same screen throughout a whole edition without removing the stencil, painting in the resist areas stage by stage between the printing of each different colour. (See plates 3, 4, 5 and 7 in colour.) As you proceed the open areas become smaller and the final stage may be printed over many layers of colour (see plate 11c in the colour section).

If you are going to stick to a definite pre-planned design, you must have every stage very clearly thought out. It is easy and infuriating to make the mistake of blocking out the wrong bit. On the other hand this method of stencil-making does lend itself to experiment. You may want to improvise and work spontaneously, letting each stage suggest the next as you go. The main thing to remember is that you cannot easily reclaim a blocked out area without making a mess.

A flat bristle brush can be used for applying the glue to a large area and finer water colour brushes for more precise detail. Or if a very large area is to be covered, raise the screen slightly and use a piece of card or a squeegee or coating trough to scrape the glue across. When using a coating trough, tilt the screen to an almost upright position (figs. 45a and b). The glue will probably need diluting with a little water, especially when a soft brush is being used.

For the mesh to be immaculately blocked, you may need more than one coating of glue. Hold the screen up to the light to detect any pin holes or thin areas. Turn the screen and paint on the reverse side. When the screen is adequately covered, leave the glue to dry thoroughly in a warm place or use a fan heater to speed up drying. The screen must lie flat while drying so that the glue does not drip down the mesh.

At intervals during the printing process, when the ink has been cleaned off, check the screen in case the resist has worn a little and apply more glue if necessary.

Do not apply the glue too thickly. Lumps and ridges will prevent the ink from spreading evenly. When the stencil is finished with it can be washed off very easily with warm water after removing the ink.

Glue and tusche. This is a refinement of the above method, also for use with oil based inks. When the glue is used in the way already described it is very difficult to produce a satisfactory fine line; the line itself cannot be drawn as the painted resist is *negative*. There is a way, however, in which a fine line can be produced; this is in conjunction with another medium, lithographic ink (also known as tusche).

The tusche is drawn onto the top side of the screen first, in the positive form of the image (fig. 46). It has a very pleasant consistency and can be painted on to the screen with a soft brush. It is soluble with white spirit. When applying it, make sure the mesh is properly filled and check for pin holes. When the tusche is thoroughly dry, pour some glue onto the screen just outside the printing area, and with a piece of stiff card or coating trough scrape the glue across,

46. Painting a positive image with tusche on to the top side of the screen.

47a. The painted tusche image.

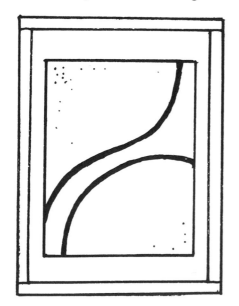

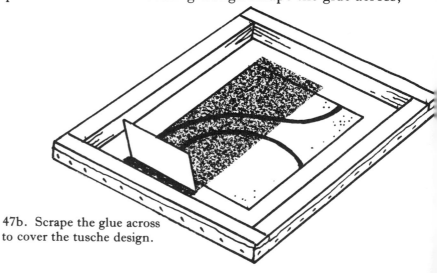

47b. Scrape the glue across to cover the tusche design.

48. When the glue is dry, rub the tusche away from the underside of the screen with a rag dipped in white spirit.

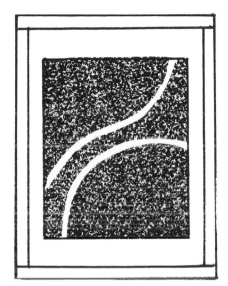

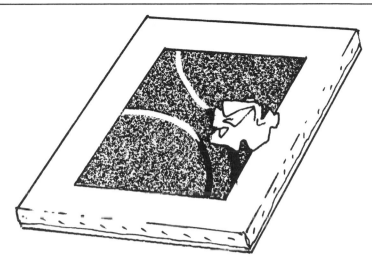

49a. The white spirit dissolves the ink and the drawn image is left as an open area through which to print.

covering your tusche drawing on the way. This can be done all in one movement, or systematically in strips (fig. 47a and b). Dry and if necessary, repeat the process on the *same* side.

When the glue is dry take a piece of rag soaked in white spirit and gently rub the areas covered by the tusche from the *underside* of the screen. The spirit, which does not affect the glue, will dissolve the ink, and the film of glue which has been prevented by the tusche from penetrating the mesh will come away easily, leaving the drawn image as a clean open area through which to print (figs. 48, 49a and b).

Melted wax and wax crayon (both soluble with white spirit) can be used in the same way as an intermediary stage to produce a positive print. (See below, melted wax and wax crayon stencils.) It must be remembered that when you use this two-stage method the stencil cannot be developed by building up on the same screen. A new screen will be needed for each colour.

Melted wax. Melted wax, which is water resistant (soluble with white spirit) can be used on its own as a block out for fabric and other water soluble inks. It is more difficult to handle than other liquid stencil materials, but it has a distinctive and beautiful character of its own and is well worth trying. You can apply the wax to the top side of the screen with a stiff bristle brush, or a tool called a tjanting which is used for batik. This is held by a wooden stem, to the end of which is fixed a reservoir with a tube-like spout at the tip. The tjanting is dipped into the hot wax, filling the reservoir, the wax then runs out of the tube, forming a fine line as you move it along the surface of the screen. The width of line varies with the size of the tube. Dots can also be made with the tjanting (fig. 50).

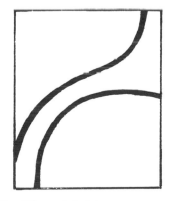

49b. The printed image.

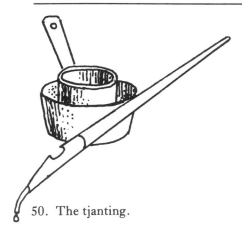

50. The tjanting.

Old candle ends can be melted down for use in this way. Melt the wax over boiling water either in the top of a small double saucepan or in a tin inside a saucepan of water. Experience will teach you how hot to have the wax – the hotter it is the easier it will be to manipulate. Maintain the temperature of the wax by keeping it over simmering water and working as near to it as possible. Hold a piece of paper or rag under the brush or tjanting as you move to and from the point at which you are working so that wax does not drip on to other parts of the mesh. Do not let any thick blobs form – if there are any, scratch them off, for they will interfere with the even spreading of the ink.

Shellac (also known as button polish). Shellac is water resistant and soluble in methylated spirits, although when dry it is virtually impossible to remove from the screen. It is used with water soluble inks on screens that have to be waterproof, but it is pointless as a stencil for oil based inks.

It has a very pleasant consistency, is easy to apply with a brush and is very quick drying. Dilute it with a little meths if necessary to make application easier. Examine the mesh for pin holes – two coats might be necessary. Heat will soften the shellac, so do not put the screen too close to a source of heat.

As with the glue method, it is possible to build up a stencil in several stages on the same screen. Tusche and wax can be used as an intermediary stage (see p. 36, glue and tusche) because shellac is not affected by white spirit.

Wax crayon. Wax crayon or dry candle can be used to draw on the top of the screen and used either on its own as a resist for use with water soluble inks, or as an intermediary stage in conjunction with glue or shellac. (See plate 19, no. 4.)

Wax rubbing. If wax crayon or candle is applied to a screen placed over a textured surface, interesting textures will appear on the screen. (See page 76, textures.)

4. Photographic stencils

All the effects produced by other types of stencil described in these pages can be achieved by photographic means, but the scope also extends far beyond this. Finer, more detailed work is possible, and there is enormous potential in making use of photographs.

A photostencil can be made with the minimum of apparatus. There are four main steps: the screen mesh must be covered with a sensitised material; a positive version of the image must be made on a sheet of transparent film, the positive areas being opaque; the sensitised screen must be exposed to the positive image in strong light; and finally the photographic image is developed in cold water. Photographic stencils can be used with all types of ink.

1. Sensitising the screen. It is most important that the screen is absolutely clean – manufacturers usually recommend a special preparation to use before the sensitised material is applied. The easiest and most economical sensitised substance to apply is a liquid emulsion, which is obtainable from specialist suppliers. The emulsion can be coated on in the same way as other liquid stencils, with a piece of stiff card or a coating trough. (Do not use a brush as this will not coat evenly enough.) Apply the emulsion to both sides of the screen, removing any surplus with the edge of the trough or card. Evenness of application is important because the thickness of the emulsion will affect the light exposure requirements – the thicker the emulsion, the longer will be the exposure needed to harden it. Obviously, the thickness of the coating must be consistent all over.

The screen should be held upright while it is being coated (fig. 45b) and then laid horizontally to dry. A fan heater may be used.

There are also various film materials which can be attached to the mesh instead of coating it with emulsion, and the advantage of these is that perfect evenness is achieved. Sawtooth edge, which might occur with liquid stencil, is avoided. Some types of film are pre-sensitised, others have to be sensitised before application. Some can be exposed before they are attached to the screen and stuck on later. However it is not practicable to discuss fully all the types of film that are available – and many of them are really more suitable for use in commercial and industrial screen printing. The liquid emulsions are more usually recommended for home or classroom use.

All coating materials are sensitive to blue and ultra-violet light, and all handling before exposure should take place away from daylight, using only ordinary low-wattage household bulbs.

2. The positive. The positive, opaque image will protect the sensitised area of the screen from the light to which it is exposed. The exposed emulsion will harden and remain firmly bound to the mesh while the protected, unexposed image will remain soft and wash out, forming an open area through which to print.

Transparent positive photographs can be made and enlarged as required (see no. 7, plate 19). This must be done by a professional photographer, or at least someone with the necessary equipment and experience. The photographer can also make tone separations – that is, a picture can be broken down into its gradations of light and dark, each of which is reproduced on a separate transparent sheet. (See plate 2 in colour section.) Each one becomes the positive basis for a separate stencil. Half tone (in grades from fine to coarse) and grains can also be produced by the photographer. Although the techniques do not come within the scope of this book, it should also be mentioned that it is possible for the photographer to make colour separations.

Special transparent film (Kodatrace) can be drawn on with ink or wax crayon (on the matt side) or painted with opaque paint. Do not use ordinary felt-tipped pens for this purpose (they are not opaque). Tracing paper can also be used – this is useful for texture rubbings.

A masking film (Red Mask) can be cut out and used as a positive. This need not be stuck down, but can simply be laid straight on to the screen. Similarly, cut black paper can be used.

Objects with interesting shapes and textures such as leaves, feathers and lace can be laid straight on to the screen for exposure (see pictures on p. 41).

3. The exposure. The sensitised screen is kept away from daylight or any source of blue or ultra-violet light until it is ready to expose.

The positive is placed against the screen (on the underside) and pressed firmly against it. Perfect contact *must* be maintained through the exposure period. The light should be directed on to the underside of the screen through the positive. The inside of the screen must be blocked up, so that no light can penetrate from another direction.

The best device for this process is a deep light-box, large enough to support the screen, with a suitable lamp placed inside it. The open top of the box is covered with a sheet of glass. The positive is laid on top of the glass, right side up, with the screen on top of the positive. A heavy, flat object, such as a large book or a pile of books, is placed inside the screen to keep the mesh firmly pressed down on to the glass with the positive sandwiched between. Sand bags are also excellent for this purpose.

If you are not using a box, the arrangement can be reversed. Lay the screen, underside uppermost, on a flat surface and place something solid and flat inside it. Put the positive, right side down, on to the screen, and lay a sheet of

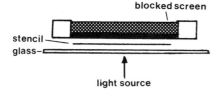

51. Section of arrangement for exposure. Perfect contact must be maintained between screen mesh, stencil and glass.

Developing the stencil by washing out in cold water. The image will appear as a clear, open area.

The leaf image on the screen.

The actual leaf used.

glass over it. Check that the contact between screen, glass and positive is adequate and expose to light from above.

The lamp most usually recommended for home and school use is a mercury vapour lamp. This is cheaper than the more sophisticated ones used in industry; the exposure time is relatively slower than most other lamps, but even so it is only a matter of minutes – photostencil emulsions take roughly 4–5 minutes.

It is most important when using a lamp of this kind to read carefully and follow the manufacturers' instructions, particularly with regard to wiring and connecting up. Also, remember that the light can seriously damage your eyes and should *never* be looked at directly. Arrange the switch so that you can be out of the way before the lamp is turned on. Exposure times may vary slightly according to circumstances including the distance of the screen from the lamp and the thickness of the screen coating. Again, consult the manufacturers' instruction leaflet.

Finally, it *is* possible to expose the screen in daylight perfectly successfully, but it is difficult to be sure of getting the exposure time right. It will take longer than when the screen is exposed to a lamp – the length of time could be anything between a few minutes and up to two hours, depending on the intensity of the light. However, it is well worth doing some experiments. The screen should be exposed underside up.

Under-exposure will result in the exposed coating washing out or breaking up after only a short run of printing. Over-exposure will result in unexposed parts not washing out. An uneven coating may result in only part of the image washing out. Make sure that the sheet of glass is very clean – marks or dirt on it will appear on the stencil.

4. Developing. Place the screen in a sink or bath and spray from both sides with cold water. After a few minutes the image will appear as a clear, open area. (See pictures on this page.) Dab the surface of the screen with a soft, absorbent cloth – a chamois leather is best – to remove surplus moisture. Do not rub roughly. Lay the screen horizontally to dry. If the screen is to be used for long runs for fabric printing, varnish it as described on page 59.

Removing the stencil. To remove the stencil after use, first clean off the ink. Manufacturers recommend special cleaners and strippers. Over-exposed stencils may be hard to remove. Finish off by spraying the screen thoroughly with cold water. A varnished screen cannot be reclaimed.

5. Improvised stencils

All sorts of materials, provided they will adhere to the screen, are thin enough, strong enough and compatible with the ink used, can be adapted for use as stencils (see p. 75, using techniques creatively).

Sticky-backed paper or tape can be stuck to the underside of the screen. For oil and other non water soluble inks use a water soluble gum-backed paper (gum strip, masking tape). For water soluble inks use a waterproof tape. You can build up a print in several stages on the same screen without removing the stencil material, but do not allow layers of stencil to build up and become too thick. (See plate 15, no. 5)

Powder. French chalk or talcum powder can be scattered on to the printing surface. This will be picked up and stuck to the screen when the first print is taken. It does not remain stable and the appearance of successive prints will gradually alter. However, up to ten nearly identical prints should come out. The printed area will feel slightly rough to the touch, as some of the grains of powder bound in the ink will stick to the printing surface. Powder can be used with oil or water soluble inks. (See no. 7, plate 15.)

Flat objects such as dried leaves, lace, or strips of raffia can be laid on the printing surface and picked up by the screen at the first printing. (See plate 19, no. 3.) The object must be paper-thin or the image will not print well – the ink will bank up around a thicker object and form a tide mark. Also, thicker items do not adhere to the screen so satisfactorily, and may drop off. Sometimes it is advisable to stick the object to the screen with a dab of glue or some sticky tape if the material (a strip of lace, for instance) extends to the edge of the printing space.

Nail varnish is soluble in acetone, and can be painted on to the screen and used with oil based or water soluble inks.

6. Guide to choosing stencils

The first and vital consideration is that the stencil and ink should be compatible – that is, the inks and their solvents must not break down the stencil material being used. However there are usually alternatives to choose from when it comes to selecting the most suitable stencil for any particular purpose. Sometimes a combination of different stencils is desirable. The following is a recapping of some of the above material, and it is suggested that it is read in conjunction with the section on using the techniques creatively (p. 75).

1. For printing large areas or simple shapes use a paper stencil, cutting duplicates if necessary, as when water soluble

inks are used.

2. For a more complex geometrical design, or where there are disconnected 'islands' of stencil, use a cut-out film that can be stuck on: Profilm, Greenfilm, Autocut or Red Mask as appropriate, according to the ink being used.

3. For a design that is informal and fluid, with curves and irregular shapes, use liquid or photographic stencils.

4. For a fine line drawing use the tusche-glue or tusche-shellac method or photographic stencil.

5. For a textured effect use liquid stencils, either on their own or in conjunction with candle or wax crayon; improvised material, such as powder; suitably treated paper; photographic stencil.

6. For one-off prints use paper whenever possible and improvised stencils.

7. For a long run of repeats for textiles, or paper prints using water soluble inks, use a strong film stencil such as Profilm or Red Mask; shellac painted on in liquid form; photographic stencil. All screens should be reinforced with varnish (see p. 59).

8. For a large edition of paper prints, using oil based inks, use any of the standard stencils appropriate to the ink – paper, film stencils, glue and photographic stencils – but avoid flimsy paper stencils and the less stable improvised materials.

9. For building up a print in stages, using the same screen without removing the stencil, use liquid stencils or gummed paper.

10. For lettering, use stick-on lettering (Letraset) in conjunction with a photographic stencil.

7. Sealing the screen and forming the ink well

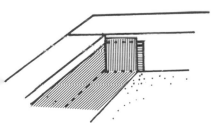

52. Wet the gum strip and stick it down to seal the angles where the mesh meets the frame, on the inside of the screen.

The screen must be sealed along the angles where the mesh meets the frame on the inside. To do this, use 5 cm (2 in.) gum strip (this is simply a brown paper strip backed with water soluble glue, and is obtainable from most stationers). Cut four strips to bend into the angles and long enough to turn a little way round the corners. Slit the ends to facilitate a neat fit round the corners. Wet the gum strip evenly and thoroughly and stick it down (fig. 52). Apply four more strips onto the flat mesh to overlap the first layer (fig. 53). Add at least one more strip to the top and bottom ends of the screen to form the ink well and some extra safety margin (fig. 54). Turn the screen over and apply more gum strip along the lines where the mesh meets the frame, for extra protection (fig. 55).

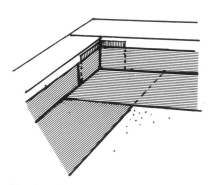

53. Apply overlapping strips on to the flat mesh, one for each side.

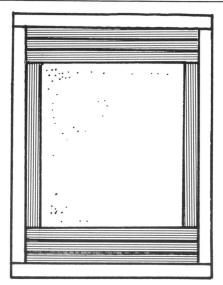

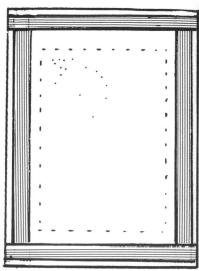

54. Add at least one more strip to the top and bottom ends of the screen to form the ink well.

55. Turn the screen over and apply more gum strip along the lines where the mesh meets the frame.

The screen should lie flat while the gum strip dries – if it is stood up on end the dissolved gum might trickle into the mesh and block it. Speed up the drying by placing the screen in a warm place or use a fan heater. As the gum strip dries it shrinks, so you will notice an increase in the tautness of the mesh.

Gum strip needs no further treatment unless water soluble inks are being used, in which case it must be waterproofed (p. 59, preparing the screen). It is very strong and will survive many printings and cleanings with strong solvents without having to be renewed.

8. Completing the blocking out of the screen

The stencil material will not necessarily cover the entire mesh – it would be a waste of expensive stick-on film to use it as a block out beyond the design area. Gaps may remain between the edge of the stencil and the gum strip. A small gap can be covered with more gum strip, but if too much of the mesh area is covered with gum strip it may cause the screen to warp as it dries and shrinks. There are better methods of blocking out.

If oil based inks are being used the gaps can be filled with water soluble glue, or paper can be taped on or stuck with a few dabs of glue. When using water soluble inks, fill in the spaces with shellac or varnish.

9. Forming a straight edge round the picture space

Draw on to the mesh, using a soft pencil, the rectangle defining your picture space.

The gum strip method: Turn the screen so that the underside is uppermost and apply the gum strip exactly against the drawn line. Turn the screen over and apply more gum strip 1 cm ($\frac{1}{2}$ in.) back from the edge of the rectangle (fig. 56a and b). Never use the strips stuck to the inside of the screen as edges – they will be damaged by the action of the squeegee.

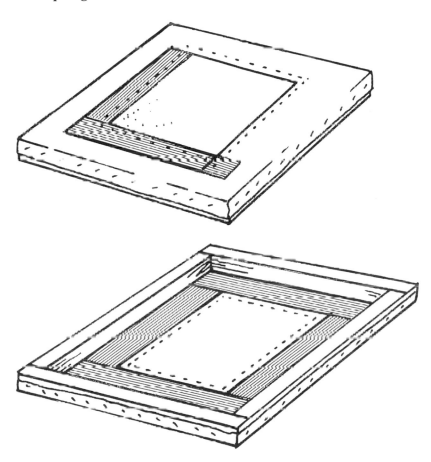

56a and b. Apply gum strip to form a straight edge round the picture space.

The glue method: This is a more reliable method for an accurate straight line as the gum strip has a slight tendency to warp when drying. The glue, being embedded in the mesh, will not peel or tear.

Stick some waterproof tape (Sellotape or Scotchgard, etc.) along two opposite sides *inside* the rectangle (fig. 57a) and apply glue alongside and over the tape (fig. 57b). When the glue is drying, but is still slightly tacky and elastic, peel off the tape. If it is pulled off when too wet, the glue will run, and if pulled off when completely dry the edge might crackle (fig. 58a). Repeat with the remaining two sides (figs. 58b and c). Edges are very important, and if they become blurred or ink bleeds outside the picture space it will spoil the appearance of the print.

Block out gaps between the edge of the rectangle and the edge of the screen with appropriate material (see above).

57a. Stick tape along two opposite sides inside the rectangle.

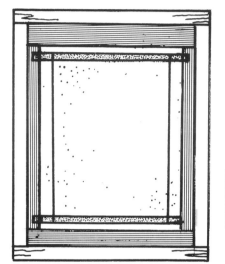

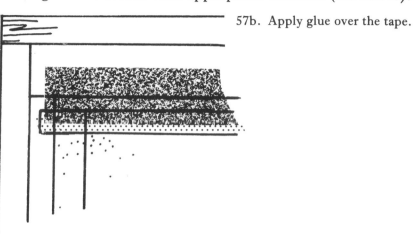

57b. Apply glue over the tape.

58a. While the glue is still slightly tacky, peel off the tape.

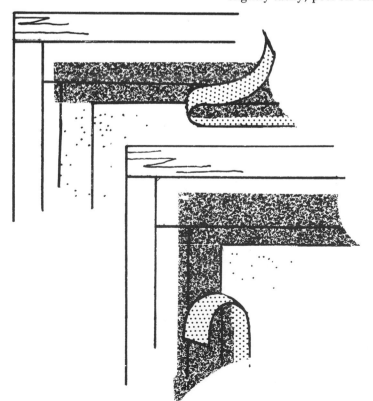

58b and c. Repeat with the remaining two sides.

Part 3
The Printing Process

1. Printing on Paper

1. Registration of paper prints

After the stencil has been put on to the screen, and the screen attached to the baseboard, the exact position of the printing paper must be established. This will be according to where on the paper you want the printed image to appear.

Place your master design, or a tracing of the image now on the stencil, in the required position on one sheet from your pile of printing papers, all of which are identical in size. Lay this on the board, bring down your screen and shift the printing paper about until the image on the screen is in alignment with the image on the paper beneath (fig. 59a and b). Raise the screen and mark the board carefully around one bottom corner of the printing paper. This is your registration mark. Each subsequent piece of paper will be placed in alignment with this mark. Thus the relationship between paper, board and stencil remains fixed.

If the position of the stencil is altered, or the screen changed for subsequent layers of colour, the paper will have to be re-registered.

When building up a stencil on the same screen (the glue method), it will not be necessary to re-register. When using loose paper stencils, the stencil is positioned on the printing paper *after* the registration marks have been established. (Fig. 36 and p. 31.)

To prevent the paper slipping off the registration marks, build a little barrier round the angle and another at the far end of the bottom line. This can be done with two pieces of card stuck down at right angles to each other, or three or four layers of masking tape very accurately laid (fig. 60a and b). The lengths should be about 10 cm (4 in.).

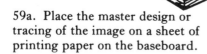

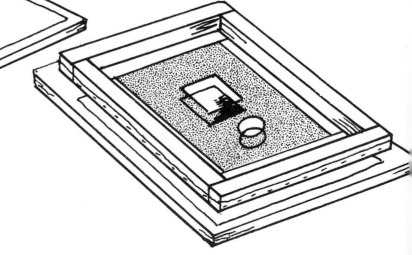

59a. Place the master design or tracing of the image on a sheet of printing paper on the baseboard.

59b. Bring down the screen and shift the paper until the image on the screen is in alignment with the image on the paper.

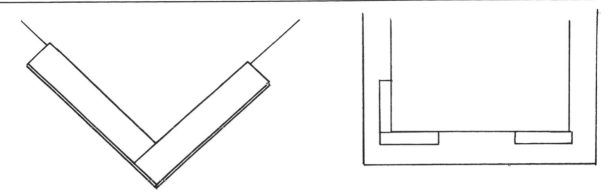

60a and b. Use card or masking tape barriers to stop paper slipping off the registration marks.

2. The design: planning the different stages

You may have a carefully planned design or you may prefer to work spontaneously. In either case, to begin with, keep it simple. If you are working to a planned design, draw it out on paper first, clearly outlining the different colour areas. Your stencils can then be traced from these shapes. The colours are printed one at a time. Each different layer of colour is called a colour separation. A separation consists of one colour, no matter how many shapes and positions it appears in, extracted from the design. Each separation will have its own stencil.

There is more than one way of printing any design. The following methods are appropriate when using paper or film stencils, directly applied stencils (with a separate screen for each colour), and photographic stencils.

1st method. The background colour (orange) is printed first through the open rectangle (fig. 61). The central shape is the open area of the stencil paper, background being blocked and the green is printed on to the orange (figs. 62, 63). For figs. 61–68 see plate 14a in the colour section.

2nd method. The green is printed first through the open rectangle, and the *positive* leaf shape is used as the resist (figs. 64 and 65). The orange is overprinted, to give the same end result as fig. 63.

The alternative chosen depends very much on the colours you intend to use. It is better to print light colours first, because even in its opaque form ink is slightly affected by the colour under it. However, this is a matter of taste – slight variations in colour can add interest to the print. The

49

choice can also depend on the nature of the design and the type of stencil used. In figs. 61–68 for example the positive and negative aspects of the design are of nearly equal weight, but with a paper stencil it would be impracticable to use a very flimsy cut-out or a lot of small 'islands' which would be difficult to position.

3rd method. The colours are separated, not overprinted at all. Print the background orange using the *positive* leaf shape as a resist (fig. 66). You now have an orange rectangle with a white central figure (fig. 67). Block out the orange background area and print the green leaf (fig. 63). This way both colours will be printed on to a white background, achieving maximum clarity.

This method needs some practice as good registration is vital. In order to avoid little hairlines of white occurring between the two colours, the second stencil should be cut with the opening slightly larger than the actual designed size, to make a small overlap (fig. 68). The smaller the overlap the better – aim for a maximum of 2 mm.

I would suggest practising with methods 1 or 2 before trying out this last one.

Try working spontaneously. For instance take a piece of stencil paper to cover the screen and cut out some shapes. This time the design will not be enclosed within a pre-made rectangle and you can work much more freely. Try tearing instead of cutting. A folded paper cut-out is a good way of achieving a very effective design, especially when one or more layers are overprinted. Try some random overprinting, and discover some interesting effects.

3. Preparing the work area

It cannot be emphasised enough how important it is to be really well organised.

Place your pile of printing paper, cut to size, as near as possible to your screen so that each new piece can easily be slipped into position for printing. For your first attempt give yourself a good chance to get the feel of printing – have 25–30 sheets of paper ready (use a cheap cartridge paper or plain news-sheet). Make sure that your drying arrangements (see p. 24, the printers table and work area) are adequate and easily accessible.

Have plenty of absorbent rag or kitchen paper in smallish pieces so that messy bits can be discarded straight

The table laid out ready for working.

away. There should be a waste-bin beside your work area so that everything you discard can be disposed of at once. It is so important to keep your hands and work area clean – the sticky ink has a strong tendency to appear where it is not wanted. Pieces of old newspaper, a little larger than the size of your picture space, should be ready as needed for clearing the screen or correcting mistakes (see p. 56, common faults – reasons and remedies).

Ink, thinners and cleaners in jars or tins to contain the mixed colours should be next to your screen on the side away from the clean paper, together with your palette, palette knife and spoon. If your screen has no supporting leg, have a small object, such as a small jar or upturned yogurt carton to slip underneath to hold it up while the prints are being removed and replaced.

You will soon come to realise how well it pays off to make these careful preparations. Mistakes generally arise when one is disorganised. There is no time during a printing session to break off and look for things. Speed, though not haste, is important. With practice a rhythm is set up so that the minimum amount of time elapses between the pulling of each print; if the ink is not kept moving across the screen it will begin to dry and clog the mesh.

One further thing to ensure is that you have enough time during which you will not be interrupted. Allow one hour for 25–30 prints – you will speed up with practice.

4. Printing

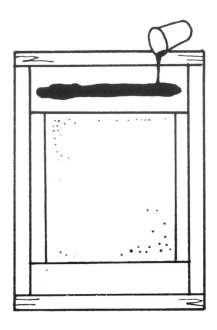

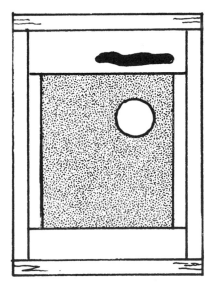

69a and b. Pour the ink into the well area and keep it topped up.

The following describes in detail the printing process where oil based inks are being used. The general procedure and handling techniques can be followed where fabric and other water soluble inks are used for paper prints, but reference must be made to the section on fabric printing (p. 59) for particular information regarding preparation of screens, cleaning up and faults, and to the section on inks for printing on fabric in part I, p. 20.

A 4 oz instant coffee jar ($\frac{1}{2}$ litre) full of mixed ink should easily be enough to print 30 open rectangles 30 cm (12 in.) square, allowing two pulls each. This can only be a rough guide. More ink will be used with a more open weave mesh than with a fine one. You will learn with experience to be more precise about the quantities to mix. In any case leftovers can usually be stored (see p. 18, inks).

When mixing two or more colours together, try out the mixture on a palette first. A piece of glass or an old biscuit tin lid make very good palettes. When you are satisfied with the colour, mix it up in a jar or old tin. Your final mixture, thinned with turpentine or white spirit to a thin cream consistency, will probably require one part thinner to two parts ink. Again, this is only a rough guide – the consistency of the ink from the tin can vary. You will only get it right by trial and error. (See p. 56, common faults, reasons and remedies). The thinner should always be added *gradually* to the ink.

When a mixture of two or more colours is being used, have two mixing jars. Make the main mixture, adding only *very little* thinner and stir thoroughly with a spoon or palette knife. A lot of stirring will be necessary to get the colours and thinning medium properly blended. Be gentle if using a glass jar – it is surprising how easy it is to knock the bottom out. Take about a quarter of the mixture, transfer it to the second jar and dilute to the correct consistency for printing. When this is used up take more mixture from the first jar and thin. (The reason for mixing in stages like this is that if you were to mix all the ink up at once with the white spirit and it proved too thin, there would not be a source of supply the right colour to thicken it with.)

If extender base is to be used for a transparent colour, this will form the main bulk of the volume of the finished

Paper being positioned in the registration marks ready for printing. Notice the pieces of card placed for 'snap-off'.

Holding the squeegee firmly, draw it towards you, bringing all the ink with it. Keep the squeegee moving smoothly. Do not stop in the middle of the print.

To return the ink to the far end of the screen, do a reverse pull holding the squeegee at a lower angle.

Raise the screen gently and remove
the print.

mixture; add the colour to it in small quantities with a little
thinner and use two mixing jars as described above. For a
rectangle 30 cm (12 in.) square pour about three-quarters of a
small yogurt pot full of ink (6 tablespoons) into the well area.
Let the ink spread across to just beyond the width of the
open space (fig. 69a and b). Always keep the pool of ink
topped up so that you do not run dry half way up a print.
You can pour in enough ink for several prints at a time, but
do not overload.

The blade of the squeegee you are using should be at
least 3 cm (1 in.) wider than the width of the open area.
Starting from the far end of the screen behind the pool of
ink, draw the squeegee straight down towards you taking *all*
the ink with it (left-behind ink will get dragged behind,
forming streaks). The squeegee is held in both hands,
positioned to give maximum control – this can be judged by
the feel and practice will get it right. The pressure should be
firm and even. Do not stop in the middle. Remember the
'snap-off' (see p. 17).

Hold the squeegee so that the blade forms an angle of
about 45 degrees with the screen. If it is held at too low an

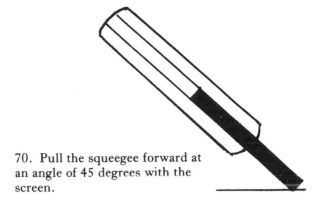

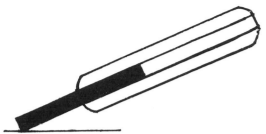

70. Pull the squeegee forward at an angle of 45 degrees with the screen.

71. Pull the surplus ink back to the well with a reverse pull, with the squeegee at an angle of about 30 degrees with the screen.

angle the pressure will not be adequate to squeeze the ink through the mesh. If it is held too upright, pressure will be uneven and the squeegee will stall and jerk (fig. 70). At the end of a pull the screen should be clear of surplus ink.

To return the ink to the far end of the screen it is easiest to do a reverse pull (fig. 71). *Don't* turn the squeegee round; you may spatter ink. Lift it to a position behind the pool of ink, knock it gently against the screen to get rid of surplus ink on the back edge of the blade and push away. Two pulls will, of course, darken the colour if you are using transparent ink. The squeegee can be held at a low angle on the way back so that less ink is forced through the mesh. If you want to make only one pull, to return, scoop surplus ink on to the squeegee and lift it carefully to the far end. In this case do not use a large quantity of ink. This movement does require a little dexterity.

Having returned the ink to the well, raise the screen gently and prop it up. Remove the print. A lightweight printing paper such as newsprint may stick to the screen, but if it needs more than a very gentle pull to remove it the ink is too thick. A heavier paper should not stick. The paper stencil will, of course, stick to the screen because the whole of its surface is exposed to the sticky ink.

It will be necessary to make a few trial prints before they look satisfactory – with a paper stencil it may take a few pulls before the stencil is firmly settled onto the mesh. The quality of the printed area will also improve. When you are satisfied, continue the process to the end of the run. The prints using oil based inks will be touch dry within an hour, but it would be advisable to wait a bit longer – two hours or more, depending on the atmosphere – before printing the next colour. As more ink is overprinted the drying time will be slightly increased. If extender (reducer) has been used this will also increase the drying time. Water soluble inks will dry more quickly.

5. Common faults, reasons and remedies

Faults inevitably occur, even to those very familiar with the screen printing process. There are so many factors to take into account. Do not be discouraged if in the first few runs the majority of the prints are unsatisfactory. This is quite usual. The important thing is to realise the cause. Some faults can be quite fortuitous, giving an unexpected effect that might be deliberately incorporated in further prints.

However for an edition of prints for exhibiting and selling it is necessary that the prints should be consistent and of a high standard.

1. Ink bleeding out of the printed area. During the first few prints, where a paper stencil is being used, this could be because the stencil has not yet settled on to the mesh. Take a few more prints on scrap paper and there may be an improvement. The most likely cause, if this continues, or if it occurs with other forms of stencil, is that the ink is too thin. Top up your diluted ink from your basic, thicker supply. If there is much ink left in the well, remove it with a spoon and return it to the mixing jar. Wipe the underside of the screen to remove the remains of the ink that has bled. Make some test prints on scrap paper before continuing with the prints.

2. Print persistently sticking to the screen. The ink is too thick. Add some thinner to the mixture in the jar. Do not add thinner directly into the well – you will not be able to judge the solution properly. Remove the thick ink from the well and return to mixing jar. There is a tendency during the course of a printing session for the ink to thicken slightly due to evaporation, so keep your eyes on the mixture and top up when necessary with thinner. When the ink in the well is replaced there is always some residual ink remaining – use a squeegee with a gentle chopping motion to mix it in with the new supply. You may also need more snap-off.

3. Little droplets of ink remaining on mesh. The ink is too thick, or maybe the squeegee is trailing a hair or thread from the edge of the mesh.

4. Printed image shows pin holes and small uninked patches. The screen is clogging. Perhaps the ink is too thick or you are being too slow. Use a screen spray, according to instructions on the aerosol can, clearing the mesh by running off a few prints on scrap paper. If you have no screen spray a controlled mixture of thin ink can be used instead to clear the mesh. Failing this, clean the screen properly as you would at the end of the session (see p. 58, cleaning up at the end of the session). If you are using fabric or other water based inks the reason may be that you are using too fine a screen mesh.

5. Ink penetrating through blocked out areas. The stencil is beginning to wear out. A paper stencil should be discarded and replaced. In the case of a liquid (directly applied) stencil the ink should be cleaned off the screen and the stencil reinforced. Repair by painting on some glue or other screen filler that is compatible with the stencils and inks being used. A photographic stencil can be repaired in the same way, using glue or shellac as appropriate.

6. Streaks appearing down the length of the printed area. The edge of the squeegee blade has deteriorated and formed little cracks. The blade should be sharpened.

7. Small blemishes appearing on the printed area. This could be caused by an unevenness under the printing paper, such as a small bit of dirt stuck between baseboard and paper. Dirt stuck to the underside of the screen will result in an unprinted or faintly printed patch surrounded by an uneven deposit of ink. Remove and take a print on scrap paper to eliminate all trace.

8. An uneven deposit of ink, like a tide mark, surrounding the blocked out area. The stencil material is too thick. This could occur when using very thick paper such as an embossed paper doily as a stencil, or an object such as a dried leaf, where the stem and veins may be too thick. Try printing on a softer, absorbent paper such as blotting paper, for better results.

9. Misregistration (misplacement of the image). Misregistration can be caused by the hinges slipping in their sockets. It can be caused by the mesh being very slack or by the misplacement of the printing paper. The latter is quite a likely cause and is seldom detectable until the second layer is being applied – so take particular care about the positioning of the new paper. If the screen is lowered too rapidly down on to the paper, the pressure of air may cause the paper to move slightly off its registration marks. Lower the screen gently and keep a finger on the paper, holding it into its registered position as long as possible.

If misregistration is only slight it hardly matters. It is up to you whether you like the effect. Slivers of background showing through between two colours which should have met can look very attractive and liven up the print. Many people allow this to occur deliberately. For a satisfactory edition however, this must be consistent and controlled.

Do not try to compensate for a registration fault by fiddling about with the position of the paper when printing the next layer. This will only lead to a progression of faults as the print develops. Make the necessary adjustment to the hinges, check that the paper is correctly positioned (there is nothing to be done about a very slack screen) and carry on. **10. A smudgy or blurred image, especially along the edges.** You probably have inadequate snap-off.

6. Cleaning up

The screen and tools must be cleaned with white spirit immediately the printing session is over. To clean the screen, first remove all surplus ink with a palette knife and transfer to a jar or tin for storing. If a paper stencil has been used this must be removed and discarded. Lay several layers of newspaper on the baseboard, lower the screen and flood with white spirit. A piece of polythene under the newspaper will protect the baseboard. Rub with absorbent rag. Remove the newspaper and repeat the process with clean paper until most of the ink has been removed. Finish off by raising the screen and rubbing with two clean rags against each other from both sides of the screen. Hold the screen against the light and check that there is no remaining ink blocking the mesh. If the ink proves difficult to remove, use a stronger cleaner (see p. 18, oil based inks for printing on paper or card). The screen should be clean right up to the edge of the frame. Deposits of ink lurking in the corners could become dissolved into the next colour.

If a fixed stencil is to be removed, the appropriate solvent should now be applied (see p. 29, the stencil). The gum strip can be removed if desired. It will in any case come off if water is applied to the screen. After the stencil has been removed, small patches of ink may be revealed which will need removing with one of the stronger solvents.

There is likely to be some staining of the mesh, but this will not affect the printing in any way.

Finally, to bring the screen to an immaculate condition and remove all trace of greasy deposits, the screen can be rubbed over with a solution of clothes washing powder, or specialised cleaning agents, recommended by manufacturers of screen inks. This final process is not always necessary, but film and photographic stencils will adhere better if the mesh is entirely grease-free.

For cleaning up after using water soluble inks see p. 71.

2. Printing on Fabric

1. Preparing the screen for fabric printing
(see p. 20 for inks)

A medium to coarse mesh should be used, because the inks dry very quickly and clog the mesh; the finer the mesh the more easily it will clog. In a highly mechanised set-up extremely fine meshes can be used, but with the cruder hand method it is not possible to achieve the necessary speed to keep the ink flowing. As inks for fabric printing are water soluble, the stencils used must be water resistant (see the stencil, p. 29).

Paper stencils should only be used for 'one-off' prints such as for blinds or individual tee shirts, because the paper quickly becomes waterlogged. Film stencils, directly applied stencils (shellac, wax, etc.) and photographic stencils are suitable for long runs and repeat patterns. Because the printing base is more flexible than with paper printing, a slightly thicker stencil can be used successfully. It is possible to use objects such as embossed paper doilies, leaves or pieces of raffia for one-off prints.

Except in the case of 'one-off' prints, the screen should be coated with varnish after the stencil and gum strip have been applied. This will strengthen the stencil and waterproof the gum strip and coat the fibres of the mesh, thus preventing the absorption of moisture from the ink (particularly important in the case of cotton organdie). Use a clear polyurethane varnish and coat the underside of the screen over the entire surface with a brush. Immediately, with a soft rag soaked in white spirit, dab the screen from the *inside* (top) over the open areas, to clear the mesh openings. Hold the screen up to the light and inspect the open areas carefully for any blocked patches. The screen should be laid flat to dry. When the varnish has thoroughly hardened, which will take a few hours, repeat the process, this time coating the *inside* (top) and clearing the mesh from the *underside*.

This process is not suitable when using a wax stencil because the white spirit will dissolve the wax. In this case use a synthetic mesh, these being less absorbent than cotton or silk. The gum strip must be varnished. When the screen has been treated in the way just described the mesh material cannot be reclaimed for further use.

2. Choice and treatment of fabric to be printed

Apart from wools, which are generally not suitable for the hand printing method, fabrics made from natural fibres are best for printing on. Cotton, linen and calico produce the best results, because they absorb the dye particularly well. Coarse weave fabrics such as hessian, and slightly textured material such as fine cotton towelling, can be printed on very successfully using a fairly open screen mesh (8x/10x) to allow the maximum quantity of ink on to the fabric. Subtle, ethereal effects can be obtained by printing on silk chiffon, which has a fine thread with a loose open weave – in which case it is best to use solid areas of colour, rather than a finely drawn design, which may get lost or fragmented on the open weave. Similar effects can be achieved by printing on fine organdie.

Silk takes more time to absorb than cotton. You will notice how much ink soaks through on to the under sheet, often producing a perfectly defined image. Being slower to absorb, so it will be necessary to wait longer between printing subsequent layers. There are inks which are particularly suited to printing on silk (Analine dyes).

Polyester/cotton mixtures will print satisfactorily. Avoid stretch fabrics and fluffy materials. Acrylics and materials with special finishes (flame-proofed and waterproofed fabrics for instance) will prove resistant to the dye colours to a certain extent. For plastic coated materials, such as PVC coated cotton, see p. 21, inks for special purposes.

Before printing, *all* materials must be thoroughly washed to remove all trace of dressings or dirt.

3. Planning a repeat pattern

72. A simple repeat, with the design contained inside rectangles with no overlap.

The size of the repeat should be worked out according to the width and length of the fabric to be printed. In a simple repeat (fig. 72) the design is contained inside the rectangle with no overlap. This makes for very simple table registration. Figure 73 is a half-drop repeat, and the registration marks will be laid out accordingly. (See p. 63, registration of a repeat pattern.)

Figures 74–76 show overlap or 'jigsaw puzzle' repeats, which means that the print will cross the registration lines. Figure 77 shows the single image as it appears on the screen.

Put as many repeats as possible on to the screen at once (fig. 78 and plate 13, nos. 4 and 5, in the colour section). This means that it will take longer to make the stencil, but it pays off in that it saves printing time, thus avoiding drying out problems, and considerably reduces the likelihood of error arising from mistakes in registration.

Inks are basically transparent (unless specially mixed with opaque white, see p. 20, inks for printing on fabric), so overprinting two colours will produce a third – this should be taken into account when planning the design. There will be a variation according to which colour is printed first.

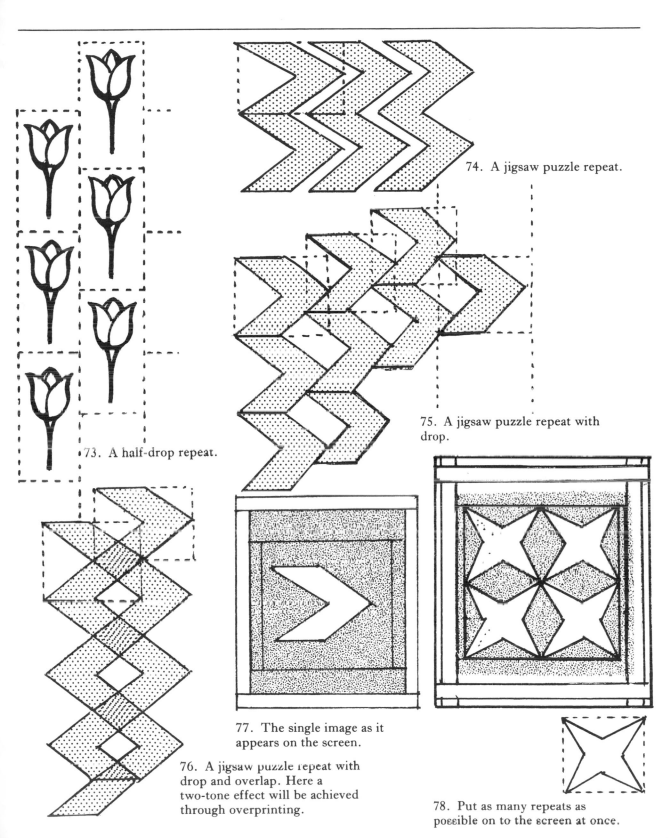

74. A jigsaw puzzle repeat.

75. A jigsaw puzzle repeat with drop.

73. A half-drop repeat.

77. The single image as it appears on the screen.

76. A jigsaw puzzle repeat with drop and overlap. Here a two-tone effect will be achieved through overprinting.

78. Put as many repeats as possible on to the screen at once.

Another thing to bear in mind is how the printed fabric will ultimately be seen – spread out as for a table cloth or bed cover, or draped as for curtains or a skirt. Sometimes a design that looks monotonous when spread flat becomes very exciting when hanging in folds. On the other hand, some designs may lose their coherence when folded.

Make some prints on tracing paper. You will need one or more for use when registering the position of the screen on the table.

4. Laying out the fabric for printing a repeat pattern

The work surface should be as described on p. 24. Over this spread an old cotton sheet, smoothed out and pinned firmly around the edges of the table with ordinary sewing pins. This will soak up surplus ink which comes through the printed fabric during the printing process.

Take the material which is to be printed and lay it straight along the length of the table, so that at least one long side and one width lie along the table edge. Pin along the edges. If the material is too narrow or short to reach across to all four sides of the table, attach the remaining edges to the table top with masking tape or double-sided Sellotape (fig. 79) (pins in the table top may damage your screen). The material should be stretched as tightly as possible. Creases should be ironed out before attaching it to the table top.

If the length of material is too long or too wide for the table, pin along the edges and let the surplus hang for the time being. If there is a lot of surplus, gather up in folds (fig. 80) and pin to the table edge.

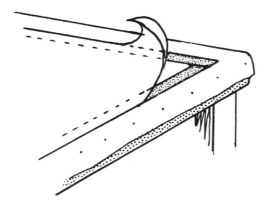

79. Attach the edges of the fabric to the table top with double sided Sellotape.

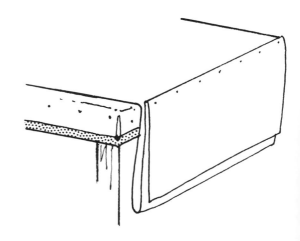

80. Gather surplus fabric up in folds and pin to the table edge.

Do not remove the material from the table until the printing of *all* the colours is complete. If it has to be done in stages, because of its size, finish one section completely. Whatever the material, there will be too much flexibility for it to be possible to re-stretch it into exactly the same position as before and distortion will occur, appearing as inconsistencies in the registration.

5. Registration of a repeat pattern

For a simple or half-drop repeat, measure exactly the rectangle containing the repeat (fig. 81a and b). Mark out these areas in lines all over the stretched fabric (figs. 82 and 83). Tailors chalk can be used for marking, as it is easily removed and is not likely to cause noticeable discolouration if it gets into the ink.

For a simple repeat, black cotton attached to pins along the table edge and stretched taut can be used to mark the lines. Positioned along the boundaries of the design it will scarcely interfere with the printing. As it is visible through the screen one can double check the position of the screen by relating the cotton line to points along the stencil. Keep an eye on the threads and make sure they remain taut and straight.

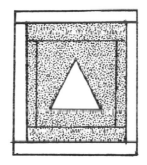
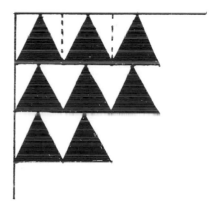

81a and b. For a simple or half-drop repeat, measure the area of the rectangle containing the repeat.

Having made a grid all over the stretched fabric, take one of the paper prints and place it in position so that the design is within the marks on the table (fig. 84). A small piece of masking tape in each corner will keep the paper in place while you position the screen exactly over the design. Now clearly mark the frame in all eight places where it touches the registration lines (fig. 85). The screen, thus marked, can now be quickly and accurately positioned over all the rectangles.

For half drop repeats using thread markers, and more complex repeats (figs. 74, 75 and 76) the registration lines

A simple repeat pattern registered with lines of black cotton.

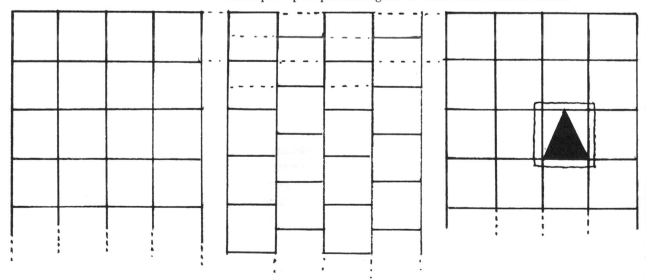

82. The areas marked out over the fabric for a simple repeat. Using chalk or thread.

83. The same area marked out for a half-drop repeat. Using chalk. If thread is used it must be re-set for the drop.

84. Place a paper print of the design in the required position within the registration lines.

For a half drop print, reposition registration lines, and again clearly mark the frame where it touches the registration lines.

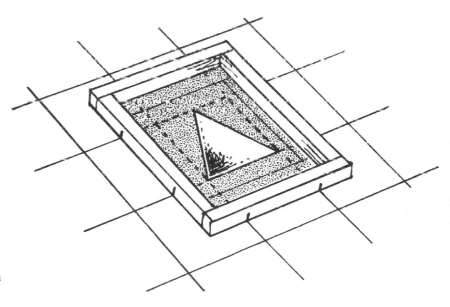

85. Place the screen exactly over the design and mark the frame in the eight places where it touches the registration lines.

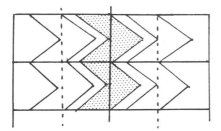

86a. Registration for jigsaw puzzle repeat shown in fig. 74. Dotted lines show second position of marking lines.

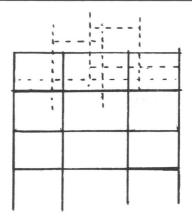

86b. Registration for the jigsaw puzzle repeat in fig. 75.

86c. Registration for the jigsaw puzzle repeat in fig. 76.

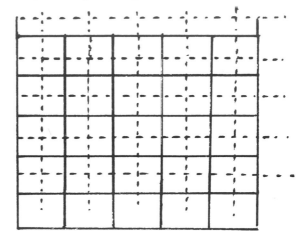

must be re-set for alternative positions of the image.

For small marks on the fabric a soft lead pencil can be used, but only in positions where it will not come in contact with the ink. If it gets into the ink it will produce permanent dirty streaks.

If the printed design is in sharp tonal contrast to the background you may be able to position the new screen for the next layer of colour simply by looking through it. Print the darkest colour first if possible. It is still advisable to mark the frame, as before, where it touches the registration lines.

If the design is not clearly visible through the screen, print a very dark version of it on white paper and use it for registration. A print on tracing paper may also be useful for positioning an overlay colour.

Another method of registration is to take a dark print on white paper, place it in the required position on the article to be printed, and place the screen over it to correspond (fig. 87)

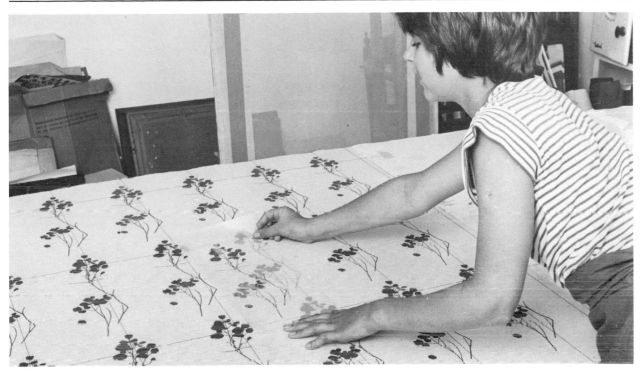

A print on tracing paper is useful for deciding on the positioning of the next layer of colour.

The screen being placed in position on the marking lines. Print the darkest colour first if possible.

Keeping one long edge of the frame on the table, swing the screen gently up, as though hinged, through a low acute angle (fig. 88). Remove the paper and carefully lower the screen back into position. Make a print, then move on to the next position. This method is easy, after a little practice, and very efficient. It can be used for an all-over repeat pattern, and is particularly suitable for small articles. When employing this method for a repeat pattern, have as many printed papers as possible positioned ready for printing. They can be kept in place with sticky tape.

87. Place a dark print in position and place the screen over it to correspond.

88. Swing the screen up gently, as though hinged, remove the paper and lower the screen back in the same position.

6. Printing a repeat pattern

Prepare the ink according to the manufacturer's instructions (see p. 20, inks for printing on fabric). It is not possible to give a precise idea of the quantities to allow as there are more variables than with paper printing. Materials vary in the amount of ink they absorb – a very thin fabric will only require one pull, medium weight cotton will take one or two, and a thick material will need at least three pulls for the ink to work into the material. The amount of ink used will also be affected by the thickness of the screen mesh. For two square metres of solid colour, printed on medium weight cotton using 8x/10x screen mesh, mix up one 4 oz coffee jar full. You can only learn through experience. Mix too much – ink can always be stored – rather than run out of a special colour which might be difficult to reproduce. The storage potential of some inks is reduced when a catalyst is added, so keep a reserve jar of mixed colour and add the catalyst only if and when the ink is required.

Have the ink, palette knife, rags, etc. conveniently near, and make sure there is a space where the screen can be laid down, if necessary, in a horizontal position and slightly raised so that it does not pick up any dirt.

It is helpful to have someone hold the screen in position while you print to prevent it slipping. When you get used to it, you will manage on your own, learning to print from quite awkward angles, sometimes one-handed. When printing a repeat, print on alternate positions so that you do not smudge the wet ink (fig. 89). The ink dries quickly and after

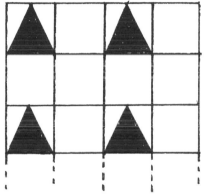

89. Print on alternate positions to avoid smudging.

Pouring ink into the well for the second colour printing.

69

You may have to print from quite awkward angles, sometimes one-handed.

a few minutes – depending on room temperature and atmospheric conditions – the printing can be completed. As a safeguard, place pieces of paper over the printed areas to avoid contact with the screen. If the ink is still fairly wet, the paper will absorb some of it, slightly reducing the colour density.

7. Printing small articles

For a series of small articles, such as headscarf squares or table mats, lay out on the printing table and fix down with masking tape or double sided Sellotape. Tee shirts can be stretched over a piece of stiff card cut a little wider than the garment, and need not be attached to the table top (fig. 90). Alternatively they can be pinned or stuck to the table, with a piece of paper inserted between the layers to prevent the ink soaking through to the back of the garment. This applies to any double sided article.

If the articles are not widely spaced out, print in alternating positions, as for a repeat pattern, to avoid smudging. Use the registration method shown in figs. 87a and b.

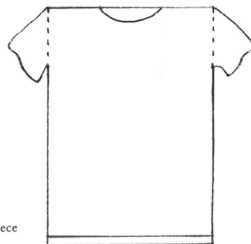

90. Stretch tee shirts over a piece of stiff card.

8. Printing 'one-off' articles

For articles such as wall-hangings, blinds or individual tee shirts, paper or other impermanent stencils can be used.

The screen must be gum stripped to seal the edges and form the ink well, but will survive the occasion without being waterproofed. Place the stencil in position on the article – a combination of stencil materials can be used together – place the open screen over it and print.

Bought ready made plain blinds can be printed on, although they have already been stiffened. However, if untreated material is being used it should be printed and cured first and sprayed with stiffening solution afterwards.

9. Cleaning up

Immediately the printing is finished, the screen must be placed in a bath or sink and thoroughly washed out in cold water. A hand spray or hose is most efficient and the ink can be loosened by scrubbing with a washing-up brush. If ink has dried on the screen it will be extremely difficult to remove and will probably need one of the special cleaners recommended for the particular brand of ink you are using.

10. Curing

After printing the fabric is left to dry for 24 hours before curing – the process by which the colours become permanently fixed.

The methods of fixing vary according to the ink product and instructions should be obtained when buying it. The most usual way of curing is by heat treatment, either by baking the fabric in a pre-heated electric oven or ironing by hand.

With the oven method, recommended times and temperatures vary from 3–5 minutes, and 140–170°C. I would suggest placing the article in a pre-heated ovenproof container, or wrapping it in foil. The oven should be pre-heated, and could be switched off once the item is placed inside.

However, I would recommend the ironing method, which most people prefer, even for larger articles, because it is more controllable. The fabric is ironed on the reverse side, section by section, for 3–5 minutes on each part. The temperature should be according to the material – if it is a lower temperature, iron for an extra minute or two.

It is difficult to give exact instructions as to time and temperature because fabrics vary so much, both in the amount of ink they absorb and the amount of heat they can take. It is advisable to make a test on a spare piece of fabric before running the risk of spoiling something on which a lot of time and effort has been spent.

In some ranges of ink, fixative is not mixed in, but is coated over the material *after* printing when the ink is dry. The material is then rolled up and enclosed in a plastic bag where it is kept moist for a few hours while the fixing solution acts on the ink. The material is then washed out. No heat treatment is required.

Some inks are self-curing, which process will take place over a number of days. Inks that require different curing methods are incompatible and must not be used together.

For the first wash after curing, the article should be immersed in a large quantity of water in order to dilute as much as possible any surplus dye that washes out.

11. Common faults, reasons and remedies

1. Printed image becomes blurred and pale. The mesh is clogging. This is one of the commonest problems in fabric printing and occurs when ink starts to dry. Perhaps you are being too slow: inefficient registration may lead to a lot of fiddling about before the screen is finally in the correct position. The mesh may be too fine, the atmosphere may be particularly hot and dry. Inks in opaque form seem to dry out more quickly. Wash out the screen with water and when dry continue printing. If there is a combination of adverse conditions it may be necessary to wash out the screen more than once during a printing session – frustrating, but worthwhile to achieve a crisp, clear image. To retard the drying, add a tiny drop of washing-up liquid – half a thimbleful to one 4 oz coffee jar full of ink.

2. Ink penetrating through blocked out areas. The stencil is damaged, or beginning to wear. Clean off the ink and repair with appropriate material.

3. Little bits of hardened ink on the screen. Ink that has been stored for a long time sometimes forms a skin which will not dissolve properly. When using old ink, strain through muslin.

4. Misregistration. This is quite often due to letting the screen slip slightly out of position, or perhaps some of the registration marks are inaccurate. Check that the material is adequately pinned or stuck down all round – it could have got pulled slightly out of position. It is important to find the reason, but do not be discouraged. Errors, particularly on an all over pattern, are never as noticeable as you think.

5. Ink spilt on fabric. Scrape off as much as possible with a palette knife. Rub the spot with cold water, taking care not to let the water spread into the design. Small spots are sometimes better left alone if there is a risk of interfering with the printed area. If you are curing by ironing, avoid these spots – they may wash out.

6. Colour washes out of fabric. There is usually some surplus dye that comes out in the first wash, but if there is a serious loss of colour, it must be that the fabric has been inadequately cured. Always make a careful note of the curing method used, for future reference.

Part 4
Using the Techniques Creatively

Blends

A very subtle way of making colour or tonal variation is by blending. Two or more colours are placed in the ink well side by side, and are allowed to merge together just enough to form a smooth gradation of colour. Use the squeegee to start working the colours together before making the first pull. After a few pulls the blend will become smoother. The position of the squeegee must not alter in relation to the pool of ink or the blend will change. Although at first your blends may not be very consistent, with some practice you will be able to produce quite a lot of identical or near enough identical prints.

Colours can be partially blended if you want a streaky effect, but it is not possible to achieve a consistent result. This could be useful for a one-off print. (See plates 10, 11 and 13, no. 3, in colour section.)

Offsetting

This is done by overprinting the same image, though not necessarily in the same colour, and shifting the registration slightly to produce a multiple image. (See plates 10 and 13, no. 4, in colour section.)

Finishes (for paper prints)

Oil based inks come in matt, satin or gloss finishes (see p. 18, inks) and can be used together in the same print. The play between gloss and matt can produce a very rich, lively effect. A matt print can also be overprinted with a clear polyurethane varnish, which is applied in exactly the same way as the ink. (See plates 4 and 5 in colour section.)

Transparent colours

Transparent colour, printed over white, looks brighter than the same colour in opaque form. It can be interesting to use the transparent and opaque version together in a subtle relationship. There are always surprises when overprinting transparent colours, and it is helpful to make a chart of overprinted colours so that a colour-scheme can be worked out exactly. When overprinting, the result may be different according to which colour is printed first – for instance a blue printed over a yellow will produce a green, but it may not be quite the same shade as that produced by overprinting the blue with the yellow. (See plates 8, 9 and 13, no. 1, in colour section.)

When making a paper print of predominantly transparent colours it is worth selecting a good quality paper, perhaps with a slight texture.

Fluorescent colours

These are useful for posters, banners, etc. and are fairly dazzling. They do not relate very well to ordinary colours, which they tend to kill. When using fluorescent inks, make the colour scheme as simple as possible and the design bold. Too many of these colours together cancel each other out. For maximum effectiveness use not more than two fluorescent colours or one fluorescent and one regular strong colour and black and white.

Lettering

Lettering can be painted on to the screen or cut out of film, but if there is to be a lot, this may not be practicable. Use a photographic stencil and either write with opaque ink straight on to the transparent film or apply stick-on lettering (Letraset) to the film. It is possible to get a reversed stick-on lettering so that it can be applied straight on to the underside of the screen. However, this is not very stable as a stencil and may last for only a few prints. (See plate 21.)

Textures

Plate 15, opposite.

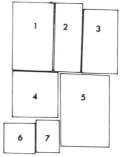

1. Print made on wrapping paper.
2. Woodgrain rubbing. This is the positive version, made using a two-stage stencil (wax and glue) and printed with oil-based ink.
3. Woodgrain rubbing, this time in the negative, printed with water based ink through the wax rubbing.
4. To make this stencil, glue was dribbled on to the screen, then spattered about by blowing through a straw.
5. Masking tape and liquid glue form the stencil for this print.
6. A wax rubbing was made from a leaf to form the first stage of the two-stage wax and liquid glue stencil used for this print.
7. In this print, powder has been shaken on to the printing paper and combed to form lines.

The purpose of a texture is to break up or soften the printed area. Screen prints are, unfortunately, often characterised by smooth flat areas of colour which in certain contexts can produce a weird, unnatural effect. A broken surface or texture helps to modify this. Here is great opportunity for ingenuity. There is usually a way to be found to produce any required effect. Textures are always created by the stencil material, either standard or improvised.

Paper stencils can be used in various ways: for a soft edge, tear the paper. Burn the edge, or burn a hole or holes in the paper. Prick holes and rub the paper with sandpaper. (See plate 3 in colour section.)

When powder is used to create a texture much depends on how it is applied. To spread thinly and evenly sift it through a fine material, such as a nylon stocking. Or it can be spread with a very soft dry brush. Scattered more thickly, it can be combed to form lines. (See plate 15, no. 7.)

Liquid (directly applied) stencils are best for forming textures: glue used in a very diluted form will provide an area speckled with pin holes, which can be very effective. Try working the glue through a piece of very coarse hessian on to the mesh. A coarse brush can be used for a streaky effect, a small stiff brush or cork can be used for stippling. A coarse comb or card with a serrated edge can be used to scrape the glue in lines across the mesh. The glue can be dribbled on to the screen or blobs can be dropped on to the screen and then blown into through a straw, so the strands of glue are splayed about in different directions. (See no. 4, plate 15.) Tilt the screen up while the glue is still runny,

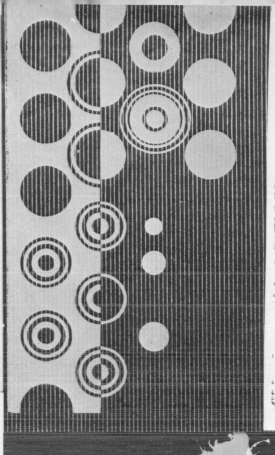

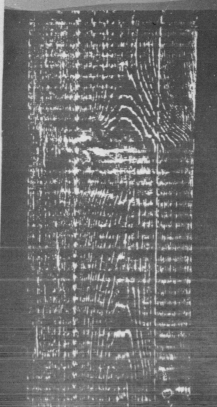
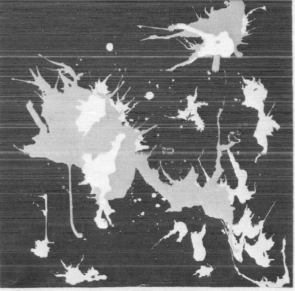

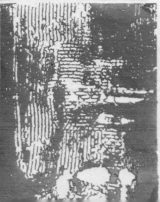

causing rivulets which change direction as you move the screen. This is not as arbitrary as it sounds, and can be controlled. The possibilities are numerous. (See plates 6 and 19, no. 1.)

Rubbings can be made on to the screen with wax crayon or a candle. (See plate 15, nos. 2, 3 and 6.) The print can either be made using the wax as a stencil, in which case the image created by the wax will be the negative or blockout, or by using the two stage method (see page 36) where the image created by the wax will end up as positive when printed.

When making a rubbing avoid anything very rough or with a sharp edge which might tear the mesh. Place the screen over the textured object and rub, using the wax thickly. Wood grain is an obvious source for textures. (See plates 1 and 22.) A few other suggestions are weathered paving stones, embossed designs on metal or other hard material, and flat objects of an interesting shape placed under the screen. Once you start thinking about textures you will tend to see them everywhere.

Monumental brasses are very good subjects and though one is not likely to have access to real ones for rubbing, there are museums and brass rubbing centres where excellent fibreglass casts of brasses are available. Keep the screen in postion on the brass with double sided Sellotape. (See plate 17.)

An object placed under the printing paper

This is not, strictly speaking, a stencil. Using the ink in transparent form it is possible to produce an image on the print of an object such as a piece of string, or lace, or folded paper, that is placed under the printing paper. Softer materials seem to produce the most satisfactory results, and the printing paper should be fairly thin. There is always a slight unevenness in the distribution of the ink surrounding the object.

Combining different types of stencil

It is often appropriate to combine two or more types of stencil in one print. For instance a print with large open areas of colour and drawn lines could combine the use of cut paper and liquid stencil as well as perhaps an improvised stencil to create a texture. (See plates 1 and 12.)

The shape of the print

Paper prints need not be confined to the conventional rectangle. Experiment by designing within a different shape, perhaps a circle, or without any formal framework. (See plates 16 and 22.)

Plate 16, top left. 'Tea at the Botanical Gardens' was made using a cut film stencil. Note the unusual juxtaposition of the objects and the informal frame shape.

Plate 17, top right. The two-stage wax and glue method was used for this brass rubbing print in white on black paper. A wax crayon was used to rub the impression of the brass on to the screen.

Plate 18, right. 'Telephone Cable' is an unusual view of an everyday object.

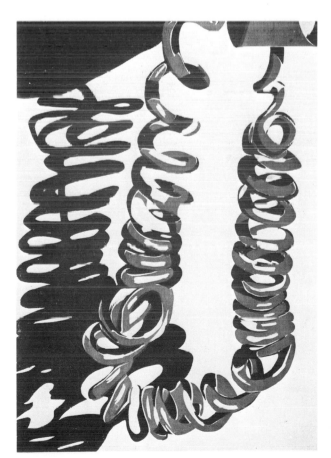

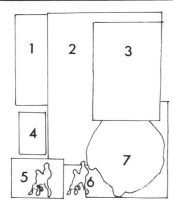

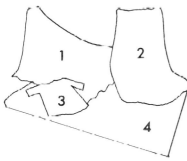

Plate 19, left.
1. Texture created by applying liquid stencil with a palette knife.
2. Design for a length of fabric. A single image overprinted in different directions creates an exciting effect.
3. Real leaves were used as stencils for this print on blotting paper.
4. Effective use of wax crayon as stencil material.
5 and 6. Positive and negative versions of this cut-out paper print. No. 5 is printed on newspaper, making use of the underlying photograph for bizarre effect.
7. Transparent photopositive made from a photograph.

Plate 20, below.
1 and 2. 'Leaf Pattern'. Two different versions of a fabric design using the same image. (See page 41 where the image appears on the screen) in different arrangements.
3. Tee shirt decorated with footballing figures. The figures were cut out of a newspaper photograph and the surrounding paper was used as a one-off stencil.
4. A cut profilm stencil was used to create this bold curtain fabric.

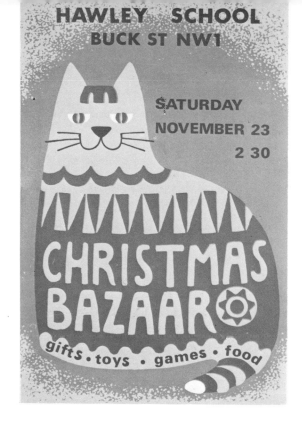

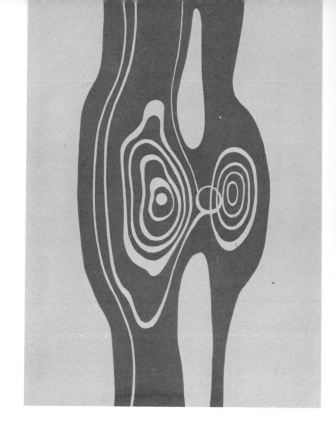

Printing cards

Small cards, such as Christmas cards, are treated like any small print. Cut the paper out to size and register each in the normal way. Do not do a number of small prints on one single page – this would create registration problems.

Printing on tiles

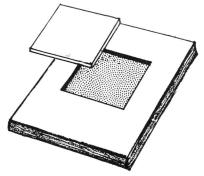

91. Cut a suitably shaped block out of an old telephone directory, and drop the tile into it.

Designing for individual tiles is a different proposition from designing a group. New patterns will form as each tile is placed against the other. Since the tile is thick the surrounding area must be built up so that the screen is lying on a flat plane, otherwise the squeegee will not pull the ink across evenly. If the size of the screen and tile are suitable, a good device is to take an old telephone directory and with a sharp knife such as a Stanley knife to cut out a wedge of exactly the area and depth of the tile. Each tile can be placed into this for printing (fig. 91). For larger tiles, build up the surrounding area with layers of newspaper. Registration is best done by sighting through the mesh. A thick line of maximum tonal contrast can be made immediately surrounding the tile. The edge can also be felt with the fingers.

Sources of subject-matter

Some media have a restrictive influence on subject-matter, but screen printing is not one of these. The wide range of style and content shown in the plates of this book is intended

Plate 21, far left. The speckled effect in this bazaar poster was achieved by letting droplets of liquid glue stencil fall from a loaded brush. A photographic stencil was made for the dark lettering and the cat's nose and whiskers using Letraset and opaque ink on transparent film (Kodatrace).

Plate 22, left. 'Woodgrain'. The first stage of the print shown in the colour section, plate 1. A print need not be confined within a formal rectangular shape.

to demonstrate this. Experimenting with the different techniques yourself will give rise to ideas for subject-matter.

The simplest beginnings often provide the best results (see plates 1, 9 and 10). A simple shape, repeated and juxtaposed in different arrangements, can produce many exciting alternatives for repeat and formal patterns (see plate 19, no. 2). In looking at design motifs from different parts of the world and from different ages, it is interesting to notice how similar the simple ingredients are. (See plate 13, nos. 4, 5 and 6.) Traditional patterns make very useful source material on which to build. Borrowing and adapting – as opposed to copying – is to be recommended and should in no way be thought of as being unimaginative or unoriginal. In seeking to be original one might sit forever in front of the blank page.

Photographs in particular are a rich source of inspiration and are easily processed into stencils (see page 38 and plate 2). Newspaper or magazine photographs can be cut out and used immediately as a stencil. (See plate 19, nos. 5 and 6, and plate 20, no. 3.)

Everyday objects, normally passed over, may surprise us once seen with an imaginative eye (see plates 16 and 18). Borrow from nature too (see plate 19, no. 3) for groups of real leaves, flower petals, feathers, etc.

A textured rubbing may be the starting point for a more developed design. (See plate 1.)

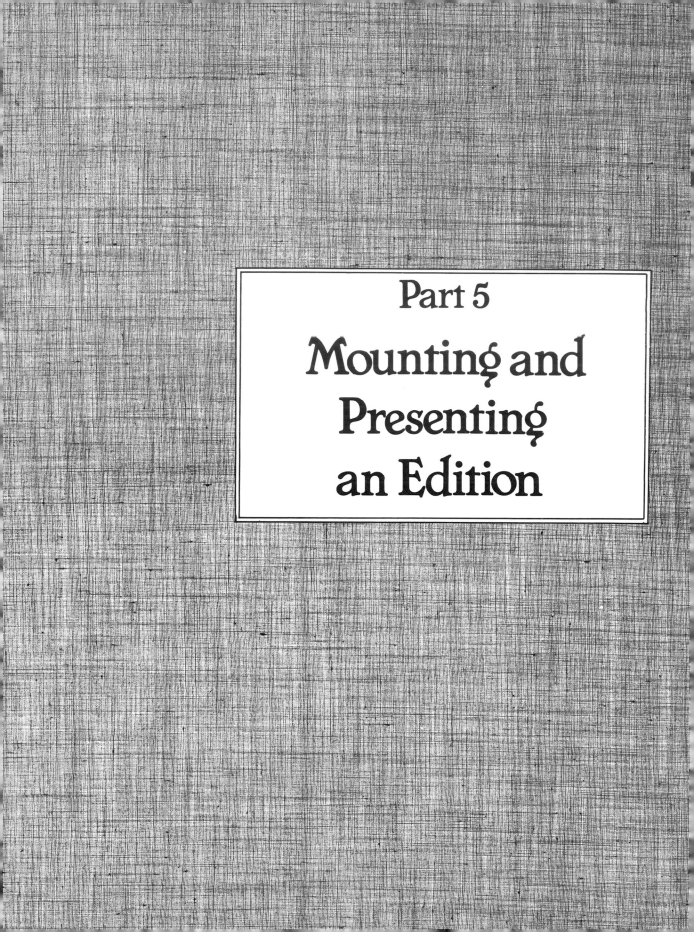

Part 5

Mounting and Presenting an Edition

When mounting paper prints, the mount should be cut at least $\frac{1}{2}$ cm ($\frac{1}{4}$ in.) larger all round than the size of the print so that all the edges are shown. Using a fairly thin card, a metal ruler and a sharp knife it is quite easy to cut a mount. Cutting a bevelled edge in a thicker card is a little more difficult, and special mount cutters are obtainable for this purpose.

If you are planning to put together an edition of prints for sale or exhibition it is essential that the prints are of a consistent standard and identical. Individual trial prints are called proofs, and an edition will be based on a satisfactory proof. The edition can consist of any number of prints, but this number must be stated, usually in the space at the bottom between the edge of the print and the edge of the mount. Each individual print is also numbered, but there is no significance as to order. So, for example, prints from an edition limited to 40 prints will be numbered thus – 1/40, 2/40, etc. The space containing this information also contains the artist's signature.

Suppliers and stockists of screen printing equipment and accessories

E. J. Arnold & Son Ltd., Butterley Street, Leeds LS10 1AX. Art and Craft products. Educational equipment.

Berol Ltd., Oldemedow Road, King's Lynn, Norfolk PE30 4JR. Art and Craft products. Educational equipment.

R. K. Burt & Co., 30 Union Street, London SE1. Paper for printmakers.

Coates Bros, Ltd., Easton Street, London WC1. Inks.

Cowling & Wilcox Ltd., 26 Broadwick Street, London W1. Folders and Polythene covers for prints, mount cutters, excellent range of stencil cutters and other accessories.

Dane & Co., 1/2 Sugar House Lane, London E15. Comprehensive range of screen printing equipment.

Dryad Ltd., 178 Kensington High Street, London W8, and Northgates, Leicester. Screen printing equipment; kits for schools, and accessories.

Falkiner Fine Papers Ltd., 4 Mart Street, London WC2. Paper for printmakers.

Keegan, Brico, Tetley Chemicals Ltd., 55 Glengall Road, London SE15. Fabric printing inks and 'Procion' dyes for silk.

John T. Keep & Sons Ltd., 15 Theobalds Road, London WC1. Inks, meshes, squeegees, and other accessories.

T. N. Lawrence & Son, 2 Bleeding Heart Yard, Greville Street, London EC1. Paper for printmakers.

E. T. Marler Ltd., Deer Park Road, London SW19 3UE. Comprehensive range of screen printing equipment and accessories.

Nottingham Handcraft Ltd., 17 Ludlow Hill Road, Melton Road, West Bridgford, Nottingham N92 6HD. Art and craft products. Educational equipment.

Paperchase Products Ltd., 213 Tottenham Court Road, London W1, and 167 Fulham Road, London SW3. Wide range of paper and card for all purposes.

A. J. Polak Ltd., 439–443 North Circular Road, London NW10 0HR. Comprehensive range of screen printing equipment and accessories.

Pronk, Davis & Rusby Ltd., 90 Brewery Road, London N7. Comprehensive range of screen printing equipment and accessories.

Reeves & Sons Ltd., 178 Kensington High Street, London W8. General arts supplies; Dryad products, screen printing inks for fabric and paper.

Selectasine Serigraphics Ltd., 65 Chislehurst Road, Chislehurst, Kent BR7 5NP and 22 Bulstrode Street, London W1M 5FR. Comprehensive range of screen printing equipment and accessories. Kits for beginners and schools.

Sericol Group Ltd., 24 Parsons Green Lane, London SW6 4H5 and 16 Nechells House, Richard Street, Birmingham B74AA. Comprehensive range of screen printing equipment and accessories.

Serigraphics, Fairfield Avenue, Maesteg, Glamorgan CF34 9LP, Wales.

Winsor & Newton Ltd., 51 Rathbone Place, London W1. General arts supplies. Screen meshes; inks for paper and fabric.

Miscellaneous items mentioned in text

Analine dyes: Keegan, Brico, Tetley (see list of suppliers).

Butt-hinges, coach bolts etc: Ironmongers.

Gum Arabic (crystals): Brodie & Middleton Ltd., 79 Longacre, London WC2.

Gum Arabic (liquid): General art suppliers.

Gum strip, masking tape, etc: stationers, art suppliers.

Kodatrace: specialist and general art suppliers.

Letraset: general art suppliers.

Light boxes and exposure lamps: most specialist suppliers of screen printing equipment.

Radial dryer: Servis Domestic Appliances, 2 Powerscroft Road, Sidcup, Kent.

Shellac (button polish) and other varnishes: general art suppliers, ironmongers, household paint and woodwork suppliers.

Solvents for oil-based ink (white spirit, turpentine substitute) and extra strong solvent for cleaning up oil-based ink (Polyclens Plus): hardware and household paint suppliers.

Tjanting: Dryad handicrafts (see list of suppliers) and Candlemakers Suppliers, 28 Blythe Road, London W8. Also some general art suppliers.

Vinyl soft covering for fabric printing table: Suppliers of furnishing fabric.

Waxed stencil paper (Wax Kraft): E. J. Arnold & Son (see lists of suppliers and stockists).

Brass Rubbing Centres: St James's Church Hall, 197 Piccadilly, London W1. St Margaret's Church, Westminster, London SW1. Also centres in Edinburgh, King's Lynn, Oxford, and York.

Acknowledgements

I should like to thank all the people who have given advice, information and help of all kinds, including the artists at the Camden Institute in London, and the pupils at Camden School for Girls, and others, who have allowed their work to be reproduced.

Individual artists are as follows:

Plate nos.

1 'Woodgrain', the author.
2 'Girls Shelling Peas', Barbara Matthews.
3 'White Cliff', Gillian Withers.
4 and 5 'Cockerels', the author.
6 'Red Planet', Alex Mullineaux.
7 'Ponte Vecchio, Florence', Kay King.
8 'Apples', R. M. Newcomen.
9 'Sunburst', R. M. Newcomen.
10 'Moving Figure', Gillian Withers.
11 'Balloon', Rita Burns.
12 'Geraniums', Zana Dene.
13 (1) 'Market Place', Katy Blee.
    (2) 'Zebras', Kate Maddison.
    (3) 'Butterflies', Fenella Freeland.
    (4 and 5) Silk squares, Jean Hunot.
    (6) Table mats, the author.
15 (1, 2, 3, 6, 7), the author.
    (4) Jessica King and Laura Maine.
    (5) Joelle de Roeck.
16 'Tea at the Botanical Gardens', Ann Kronheim.
17 'Brass Rubbing', the author.
18 'Telephone Cable', Claire du Bosky.
19 (1) Joelle de Roeck.
    (2) Gillian Withers.
    (4) Margaret Rogers.
    (3, 5, 6, 7), the author.
20 (1, 2, 3) the author.
    (4) Jean Hunot.

INDEX